BONKERS
B

SNOT

COLLECTORS
and SPIDER LADDERS

and other ~~GENIUS~~
bonkers
INVENTIONS

WRITTEN BY

Dr Mike Goldsmith

Illustrated by Clive Goddard

■SCHOLASTIC

Scholastic Children's Books,
Euston House, 24 Eversholt Street,
London, NW1 1DB, UK

A division of Scholastic Ltd
London ~ New York ~ Toronto ~ Sydney ~ Auckland
Mexico City ~ New Delhi ~ Hong Kong

First published in the UK by Scholastic Ltd, 2012

ISBN 978 1407 12453 7

Printed and bound by CPI Group (UK) Ltd, Croydon, CR0 4YY

2 4 6 8 10 9 7 5 3 1

ALL the **STRANGE,** scary and downright stupid **inventions** in this book are **REAL**

→ INTRODUCTION

The world would be a boring place without inventions. No iPods, no fizzy drinks, no shoes and no chance of reading this book either. Throughout history, as people struggled to make their lives easier, more fun, and ideally a bit longer too, some of them cleverly created all sorts of incredible and handy things. The ancient Greeks and Romans invented so many that, nearly 2,000 years ago, a Roman engineer called Sextus Julius Frontinus, even said, 'Inventions have long since reached their limit, and I see no hope for future development.' I wonder what he would have made of space stations, TVs, and chicken nuggets.

All the strange, scary and downright stupid inventions in this book are real – each was either built, patented or both. Patenting is a process by which an inventor officially informs a special organization called the Patent Office about his or her invention. This is so that if someone else nabs the idea and tries to pass it off as their own, they can be found out and prevented from using it.

Sometimes, people invent things without quite knowing whether or not they will actually be any use: when the laser was invented in 1960, people said it was 'a solution looking for a problem'. But, within a few years, it turned out to be exactly what they'd always wanted – whether it was for eye-surgery, playing CDs, getting their shelves straight or keeping time with mind-boggling accuracy.

So maybe the inventors of some of the weird and wacky gadgets and gizmos collected in this book thought they'd turn out to be useful eventually. Or maybe they just loved inventing stuff so much that they couldn't stop themselves, even though the things they came up with were totally daft.

TEN POINTLESS INVENTIONS

It's easy to see why some inventions were worth spending lots of time and effort to develop. Where would we be without TV, for instance, or toilet rolls? But there are other gadgets that really make you wonder why anyone bothered... like these:

1. Battery-powered rotating tie rack

Everyone knows adults are a) lazy and b) wear ties (well, some of them do, sometimes), but are they really too lazy to make the effort to rotate a tie rack? Just in case YOU know an adult like that, the rotating tie rack, invented in the 1970s, is the perfect gift. It rotates at the press of a button, saving Dad the bother. But you do have to wonder why those groovy 70s people didn't simply hang their ties in a row, avoiding the need to rotate anything at all. Oh wait, maybe they did and that's why this didn't catch on...

● ● ● ● ● ●

2. Edible business card

As grown-up as ties, business cards are an essential part of working life for many adults, and handing one over avoids the need to write down phone numbers (or indeed remember people's names). So long, of course, as the business card isn't later lost, stolen or ... er ... eaten. That would make it completely useless. The edible business card was made of strong rice paper, but not given any particular flavour, which might have made it more popular. Perhaps.

THE EDIBLE BUSINESS CARD

3. Battery charger disguised as a toaster with a bread-shaped battery holder

The thing with battery chargers is, they don't look very much like toasters. This is true of a lot of household gadgets of course, but the inventor of this marvellous device must have thought that battery chargers really SHOULD look like toasters. Given that batteries must on NO ACCOUNT be heated up (because it makes them explode), concealing them inside a fake piece of bread just begging to be toasted seems unwise.

● ● ● ● ● ●

4. Popcorn fork

Some foods are tricky to eat with a fork – cherries, crisps and popcorn, for instance. Some of us conclude that that's what fingers are for, but the inventor of this gadget knew better.

5. Toast personalizer

Ever had your toast stolen? No? Well, if you had, you might have wished it had your name on it. And so it would, if you'd had your own toast personalizer. They are specially shaped plastic stamps that you press briefly into the bread before toasting. The pressed-down bits don't toast as much as the rest of the slice, so your name appears in pale letters against a toasty brown background.

6. Leonardo da Vinci poseable action figure

Poseable action figures are ideal for pitting your very own version of Batman or Doctor Who against their deadliest (plastic) enemies. They are perhaps less ideal for reliving scenes from the lives of great artists. See page 17 for more on Leonardo.

7. Cordless skipping rope

If you're one of those people who is totally determined to skip while being utterly useless at it – tripping over the skipping-rope, winding it round your friends and so on – this invention is for you. If not ... it isn't.

8. Motorized ice-cream cone

Picture the scene. It's really hot and your ice cream is starting to melt. Bad enough in itself, but what if the melting ice cream is about to run down the FAR SIDE of your cone? What on Earth can you possibly do in this nightmare scenario? With a motorized ice-cream cone, your problem is solved: the motor turns the ice-cream cone around, giving you instant access at the flick of a switch. Amazing this one didn't catch on, really.

9. Expandable raincoat (to shelter a friend)

This invention is designed especially for those situations when you've remembered to pack for a possibly rainy walk and your friend hasn't (and you know they haven't and they didn't listen when you told them they should). In other situations, its use is, let's face it, a bit limited.

10. Leg puppets
Some really good inventions are a logical step forward from something that already exists. Shampoo for dogs. Vacuum cleaners for cars. Puppets for legs? (Full details opposite.)

INVENTION: LEG PUPPETS

DATE: 1924

INVENTOR: Elma Blanton

The brilliant thing about leg puppets is that they're different every time you use them. This is how to make your very own: To begin with, simply paint both your knees with little faces (getting a friend to help if you're not arty enough). Put some elastic around your legs, just above the faces, and attach small wigs and hats to it. Then, just let yourself go with the rest of your leg, adding tiny dresses, small shoes, teeny trousers – whatever takes your fancy. Elma said in her patent, 'if operators have any muscular control over the knee cap the facial expression of the puppet actors may be considerably changed at will.' Now, I have to admit that the key word here is 'if'. In fact, before you actually start tracking down teeny-weeny wigs or knitting extra-small sweaters, you might just want to draw a simple face on each of your knees and then try altering their expressions...

Before their time

To be a successful inventor, you need more than a great idea. You also have to come up with it at a point in history when it's actually of some use, otherwise you might well have to wait until you're dead before it catches on. This timeline shows just how easy it is to invent things too early.

Greece, around AD 100 The world's first steam engine, the Aeolipile, is built by Hero of Alexandria. A brilliant idea, used for ... well, nothing really. A bit of it spins around very nicely though.

Italy, about 1475 The first parachute is invented. The parachute came complete with a novel safety feature: the handlebars were fastened to your belt, so if you let go, the parachute would remain attached to you. On the other hand, given that the bit that did the actual work of slowing you down was about the size of an umbrella, it probably wouldn't have made a great deal of difference to your rate of fall if you did leave it behind. Let's hope no one actually tried it.

England, 1712 The first successful steam engine – the Atmospheric engine – is invented by Thomas Newcomen. Very useful for pumping water out of mines.

Paris, 1783 The earliest hot-air balloon trip took place – a chance to try a parachute! Though no one tried jumping out of this balloon, a parachutist did hurl himself from a similar one two years later. Luckily the parachute involved was a bit better than the 1475 version.

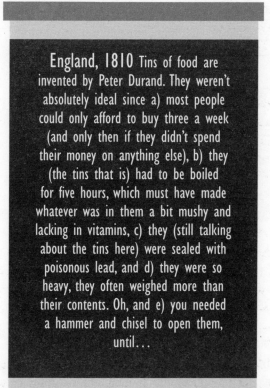

England, 1810 Tins of food are invented by Peter Durand. They weren't absolutely ideal since a) most people could only afford to buy three a week (and only then if they didn't spend their money on anything else), b) they (the tins that is) had to be boiled for five hours, which must have made whatever was in them a bit mushy and lacking in vitamins, c) they (still talking about the tins here) were sealed with poisonous lead, and d) they were so heavy, they often weighed more than their contents. Oh, and e) you needed a hammer and chisel to open them, until...

USA, 1858 The can opener is invented. Hurrah.

England, 1871 The computer (then called the Analytical Engine) is invented by Charles Babbage. In the absence of electronics (and indeed much in the way of electricity), Babbage tried to build his computer from lots of tiny little cogs and wheels, and it would have needed a steam engine to power it – if he'd actually managed to get it built. See page 4.

USA, 1917 Speech balloons are invented, for use in silent films. These were real balloons with words written on them, which the actors had to rapidly inflate at the key moment, carefully holding them up to camera at the same time as carrying on with the actual acting: fighting, shouting, waving their arms about and so on. Never mind, with such a great invention, the future of the silent film was assured...

1923 Silent films start to be elbowed about by ones that starred people actually saying things out loud.

Germany/England/USA, the early 1940s The first computers that actually work (though not all that often, as they are very unreliable indeed) are invented.

ECCENTRIC INVENTOR #1: LEONARDO DA VINCI

Leonardo was a Renaissance Man. Since he was a) male and b) lived during the Renaissance. (This was a time when, especially in Italy, there was a surge of interest in arts and sciences, inspired by ancient Greek writings.) It might seem rather obvious, but a 'Renaissance man' actually meant someone who knew everything that was worth knowing - how to draw, the latest scientific theories - such as they were, how to speak Latin, play instruments - a banjo perhaps - that sort of thing.

And Leonardo really was good at all sorts of stuff. He made world-famous paintings of the Mona Lisa and the Last Supper, and amazing drawings of the inside of the human body (based on his dissections of corpses). He also made many scientific discoveries and invented all

sorts of seriously handy
things like submarines
and flippers.

However, in most
cases, Leonardo
only thought
up and drew
his inventions
- he didn't actually
build many of them. Which
may account for the oddness of a
few of his ideas. His tank, for example,
was a strong, boat-shaped wooden shell
containing a set of large gears which were
connected to its wheels. If he'd actually built it, he
would have discovered that, since the front wheels
turned one way and the rear wheels the other, it
wouldn't actually have gone anywhere.

Then there were his flying machines. He came up
with several of these, but the main idea behind most
of them was that, by turning wheels, pedalling, or
moving levers, various wingy things would flap about
and cause the machines to take to the sky. However,
as the machines were invariably built on a massive
scale, with lots of heavy wood and leather, they could
only have worked if the pilots were about ten times
as strong as normal humans.

Leonardo also came up with some rather alarming inventions. He designed a mechanical knight which would suddenly stand up and sit down again, and came up with a set of stretchy bulls' intestines, which could be inflated as a practical joke. Supposedly, these could be inflated to a large enough size to fill a whole room - most amusing if there are unsuspecting friends in it at the time.

Perhaps his scariest invention - and it seems he did actually build this one, just for a change - was a walking robotic lion which would roar and then suddenly open its own chest, to reveal ... a big bunch of flowers. This was built for François I, King of France, for whom Leonardo was working at the time, and it was shown off at peace talks between François and King Leo X of Italy.

INDOOR SWIMMING MACHINE

- Keen on swimming but hate the water?
- Like a bit of front crawl but can't be bothered to go to the swimming pool?
- Embarrassed by swimwear you really ought to keep because it was a present from your aunty?

If any of these sound like you, this relatively new invention (patented in 2001, in Colorado, USA) is the answer.

All you need to do is assemble the machine by following the simple diagram below, attach your limbs to the appropriate bars and start swimming.

It's completely impossible to drown!

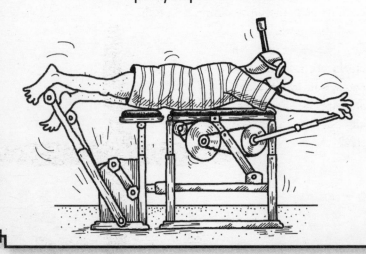

SNAPPY HEADGEAR

Long, long ago, before even your parents were young, just about everyone – ladies and gents alike – wore a hat in public. Most people saw hats as handy headgear that made a nice fashion statement while keeping their ears warm or the Sun out of their eyes. But not inventors. They saw them as ideal platforms for their latest brilliant wheezes. One such scheme was a signalling system requiring nothing more than a bubble-making device that could be attached to your favourite trilby, bowler or fedora, which would blow bubbles from your head as you walked along. Of course, you'd need to give your friends a few lessons to teach them to understand bubble-code.

Another invention, designed to save gentlemen the exertion of tipping their hats to greet ladies, was a self-tipping hat, operated simply by pulling a string. Ideal for anyone who just couldn't be bothered to do it for himself.

Or, how about a clockwork fan, to draw cooling air into the hat, and blow head-warmed-air out of the other side?

Yet another great idea was to install a camera in your headgear. A useful cape-like attachment would cover your head to keep excess light out, and a special hat-flap was used to cover the lens. A magazine called 'Punch' even published a poem about it:

If they knew what I wear when I walk down the street
I should be quite a terror to people I meet
They would fly when they saw me
And never stop to chat
For I carry a camera up in my hat

Letter to the editor

To The Editor, the London Times
May, 1989

Dear Sir,
I am writing to protest in the strongest possible terms about the recent invention of the patented 'spiked shark protector suit.' If it should catch on, and all human swimmers should begin to take to the seas protected by its vicious protruding spikes and numerous metal plates (most injurious to the teeth when nibbled), it would surely spell the end for one of the most loveable animal species. I feel sure that only the discomfort, weight, price, awkwardness, and ridiculous appearance of the suits has preventing them being used frequently – or indeed, at all – to date. However, I fear that nothing less than an outright ban will be sufficient to ensure that large marine predators can feel safe in indulging in the harmless snacking which does so much to add excitement and speed to human swimming activities.

Yours faithfully,

Mr G. W. Shark

INFOMERCIAL

International Detectives' Monthly
December 1930

Once again, science has come to the rescue of detectives everywhere; this new invention seems likely to join the fingerprint revealer, the lie detector and the very large magnifying glass in the list of essential crime-fighting instruments.

The device is designed especially to work with the more nervous type of criminal. The detective sits inside a large box with a window in the front, which is equipped with a concealed microphone and camera. But all that the suspect under investigation can see is a COMPLETELY TERRIFYING SKELETON. The detective's voice emerges from the skeleton's mouth and the camera makes its recordings through its eyes.

All the detective has to do is put on a suitably frightening voice, and outline the ghastly vengeance that the skeleton will enact on any criminals who don't confess their crimes. The suspect's guilty conscience will do the rest: their prompt confession will be recorded by the hidden microphone and camera.

NOTE: in order to avoid terrifying your colleagues and innocent members of the public, it is recommended that the COMPLETELY TERRIFYING SKELETON is returned immediately to its box after use. The manufacturer can accept no responsibility for any non-criminals who are inadvertently terrified by this product.

THOMAS BEST'S PATENTED
BEAUTIFYING CHEEK-PADS

Congratulations, you've made the right choice! As the proud owner of a pair of our inflatable cheeks, you need never worry about looking thin-faced or wrinkly-cheeked again. The cheeks are comfortable, safe and – most importantly – completely undetectable*. Simply inflate, insert the bungs (provided), and place them in your mouth. Friends and relatives will hardly believe how full, smooth, and altogether bulgy your whole face is.

**If it doesn't say Best on the box,
it's not Best in the box.**

* If the user does not speak, eat, drink, or open his or her mouth.

ARE YOU TIRED OF PICKING FOOD
OUT OF YOUR DOG'S EARS?

HAD ENOUGH OF BEING EMBARRASSED IN FRONT OF
VISITORS WHEN YOUR PET DIPS THEM
IN HIS OR HER LUNCH?

BORED OF HOLDING BACK CANINE EARS MANUALLY WHEN
STEW IS ON THE MENU?

If so, look no further than our patented
ear-protectors. Simply clip them over Fido's ears just
before meal time and you'll never be embarrassed
by your dog again. That's not all … in a range of
attractive colours and with a wipe-clean surface,
they're canine fashion accessories, too!

EAR-PROTECTORS.

If your pet could speak, he'd thank you.

IF AT FIRST YOU DON'T SUCCEED...

Inventing things is rarely easy. Almost all inventions went through a long and irritating period of development – often by many different inventors – and a series of not-very-good early models before the successful version that everyone had been waiting for was built. In some cases, we're still waiting...

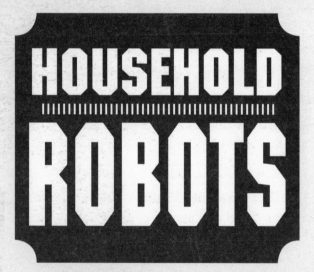

If there's one thing most people don't like, it's housework: making beds, ironing, cleaning ovens – it's just no fun. Of course, if you have pots of money you can get someone else to do it for you, but everyone else just has to do it themselves, unless they can get their mum or dad to do it for them. Or do they? People have come up with some brilliant machines over the centuries, and few are more brilliant than robots. They do all sorts of things fantastically well and are far better at some jobs than we are - such as car-building, underwater maintenance and space exploration (robots have visited every planet in the solar system, not to mentions several comets, asteroids and moons, while people have only got as far as the Moon). So why not get a robot to do the housework? What a great idea!

Of course, some household tasks have been done by machines for a long time. Dishwashers, washing machines and toasters were all very handy and people were quite pleased, but it wasn't QUITE what they had in mind. What they really wanted was something that could make beds and make tea, let the cat out and wash the windows, lay the table and cook the dinner, do the ironing and remind you to wear a tie, bath the baby and tidy up after itself. A fully functional, reliable robotic servant.

Robots really got going in the 1960s (with UNIMATE, a robot that worked in an American factory, moving hot bits of new car around), and it wasn't long before science magazines and TV shows were featuring robots that would be doing the housework sometime soon.

Sure enough, prototypes of these robotic servants were soon being built.

First out of the lab, in 1966, was Tinker, which could vacuum the carpet and wash the car. Excellent? Well, kind of, but it took absolutely ages to use, because it had to be given a vast series of exact instruction first: 'Move cloth up 5 cm, then 25 cm to the right' ... that kind of thing, over and over again. It usually took about four hours to input the whole series. Even to wash the same car a second time, Tinker needed to be positioned exactly right, or it would wash the air instead.

Then, in 1976, there was Arok. For some reason its inventor gave it a scary face inside a kind of space helmet, which must have put off those few people who weren't already startled by its terrifying price: $57,000, which meant it cost a lot more than the houses it was supposed to be cleaning. Arok could vacuum and serve drinks too. Though not actually very well.

The trouble is, houses aren't designed for robots. They are full of tricky obstacles like closed doors and stairs. They're also full of human beings, who are delicate and easily damaged, and children, who can easily damage robots. Even getting a robot simply to crawl around on Mars looking at things without falling off precipices is a challenge.

The other problem is, it can be hard to get a robot to do exactly what you want. It's fairly easy to get a robot to unroll a duvet on to a bed - if you give it the duvet. If the duvet is on the floor somewhere and the robot is expected to find it, the only way it can do so is by spotting that it IS a duvet - which means it has to understand what a duvet is, what happens when you move it in various ways, and what it's used for.

In other words, it needs to understand the idea of a duvet - but no one knows how to build a robotic brain which is able to understand ideas like this. As it is, instructing the robot to find the duvet would be like explaining how to do something without using nouns. Just think of telling someone how to change a duvet cover using words like 'lift', 'pull', and 'grasp' without like 'duvet', cover' or 'button'. You might find that even more annoying than actually changing it yourself.

The only jobs household robots can do are simple repetitive tasks that don't require any understanding of the things around them - which is why today's household robots are pretty much limited to vacuum cleaners, floor-washers and mowers. And that's not likely to change any time soon.

A MULTITUDE OF MOONSHIPS

People have been gagging to go to the Moon ever since they worked out it was real (and not, say, a reflection of the Sun, as was once imagined). Many people came up with bonkers ideas about how to get there. Here are some of the earliest – written in books and poems – most of which are rather hopeless:

MOON VEHICLE: **Giant waterspout**
INVENTOR: **Lucian of Samosata**
NATIONALITY: **Greek**
SUGGESTED IN: **True History**
DATE: **2nd century** AD
NOTES: The two problems with this one are a) you can't decide when to go to the Moon, you simply have to float around in your ship waiting for a handy 'waterspout' to whisk you off there, and b) there are no such things.
ORIGINALITY: **1 out of 10**

MOON VEHICLE: **One eagle's wing plus one vulture's wing**
INVENTOR: **Lucian of Samosata**
NATIONALITY: **Greek**
SUGGESTED IN: **Icaro-Menippus**
DATE: **2nd century** AD
NOTES: The idea here is that big strong birds must have wings that are great for flying. Which they do, but you kind of have to be a big strong bird yourself to use them. Even then, you couldn't fly without air, and there isn't any air between Earth and the Moon.
ORIGINALITY: **2 out of 10**

MOON VEHICLE: **Throne with meat and eagles attached**
INVENTOR: **Firdausi**
NATIONALITY: **Persian**
SUGGESTED IN: **Book of Kings**
DATE: **1010**
NOTES: The meat was just out of reach of the eagles, who would fly towards it, pulling the throne with them. You can try this one for yourself, just try pulling yourself up into the air by your shoelaces, just to see how well it works.
ORIGINALITY: **4 out of 10**

MOON VEHICLE: **Horse-drawn chariot**
INVENTOR: **Lodovico Ariosto**
NATIONALITY: **Italian**
SUGGESTED IN: **Orlando Furioso**
DATE: **1516**
NOTES: This one would be ideal if there was a road to the Moon, with gravity, air, and some horse-friendly snacks.
ORIGINALITY: **0 out of 10**

MOON VEHICLE: **Demons**
INVENTOR: **Johannes Kepler**
NATIONALITY: **German**
SUGGESTED IN: **Dream**
DATE: **1634**
NOTES: Nice idea if you can find some, and they're not too scary.
ORIGINALITY: **1 out of 10**

MOON VEHICLE: **25 geese**
INVENTOR: **Domingo Gonzales**
NATIONALITY: **English**
SUGGESTED IN: **The Man in the Moone**
DATE: **1638**
NOTES: This idea, from an English science fiction story, was really the same as Firdausi's, minus the meat. Yes, good point, 'Domingo Gonzales' isn't a very English name: he was really called Francis Godwin, but he was the Bishop of Hereford, so maybe he thought writing science fiction was a bit beneath him.
ORIGINALITY: **2 out of 10**

MOON VEHICLE: **Jacket with glasses of dew attached**
INVENTOR: **Cyrano de Bergerac**
NATIONALITY: **French**
SUGGESTED IN: **Voyage to the Moon**
DATE: **1649**
NOTES: The scheme was that the dew would be drawn up into space by the Sun, taking the jacket, and its wearer, with it.
ORIGINALITY: **6 out of 10**

MOON VEHICLE: Flying box with added firecrackers
INVENTOR: Cyrano de Bergerac
NATIONALITY: **French**
SUGGESTED IN: **Voyage to the Moon**
DATE: **1649**
NOTES: This is actually the only invention in this list that would have worked — sort of. Firecrackers are a bit like rockets, which are the only known way to send a craft into space. It would have taken millions of firecrackers, though, and I wouldn't have fancied being in the box, myself.
ORIGINALITY: **5 out of 10**

MOON VEHICLE: Spring-powered catapult
INVENTOR: David Russen
NATIONALITY: **English**
SUGGESTED IN: **Voyage to the Moon**
DATE: **1703**
NOTES: Though it might have got a vehicle into space, it would have needed to reach a speed of several kilometres a second in under a second (before the craft left the end of the catapult, for instance), which would have flattened the crew.
ORIGINALITY: **6 out of 10**

MOON VEHICLE: **Rocket-powered flapping wings**
INVENTOR: **Daniel Defoe**
NATIONALITY: **English**
SUGGESTED IN: **The Consolidator**
DATE: **1705**
NOTES: A good idea to use rockets, but a bad one to use wings.
ORIGINALITY: **9 out of 10**

MOON VEHICLE: **Balloon**
INVENTOR: **Edgar Allan Poe**
NATIONALITY: **USA**
SUGGESTED IN: **The Unparalleled Adventure of one Hans Pfaall**
DATE: **1835**
NOTES: This'll never work: the air runs out a few kilometres above Earth, and a balloon can rise no higher than the air (because it has to be lighter than whatever is around it to rise — if there's nothing around it, it would have to be lighter than nothing to get any higher).
ORIGINALITY: **1 out of 10**

MOON VEHICLE: **Giant cannon**
INVENTOR: **Jules Verne**
NATIONALITY: **French**
SUGGESTED IN: **From the Earth to the Moon**
NOTES: This has the same problems as the spring-powered catapult, opposite.
ORIGINALITY: **3 out of 10**

MOON VEHICLE: **Antigravity metal**
INVENTOR: **H. G. Wells**
NATIONALITY: **English**
SUGGESTED IN: **The First Men in the Moon**
NOTES: The idea here was that, just as some substances can't be penetrated by light, or heat, or sound, there might be another one that cuts off gravity. So if you put a chunk of antigravity metal under your spaceship, the Earth's gravity wouldn't reach you or hold you down any more. Actually, gravity is a different kind of thing to light or heat — it's more like time, or mass — so it can't be cut off.
ORIGINALITY: **9 out of 10**

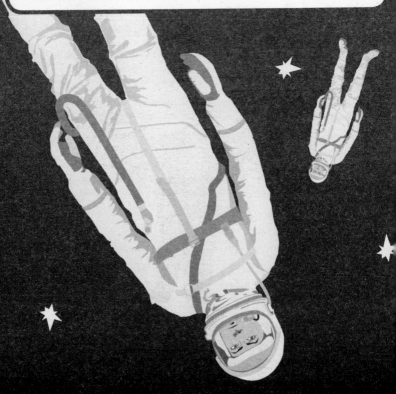

FOR THE BIRDS?

For any invention to succeed it needs publicity – but that's no problem at all if it happens to be a human-powered flying machine. There are annual competitions at which these are put through their paces – everywhere from Japan, China and Australia to Bognor Regis. These contests have been running since 1971, and they include some serious attempts to build useful vehicles. They also include a great many bonkers devices, some of which are really just an excuse to dress up as a big bird. In the Bognor Regis competition, the competitors fling themselves off the end of the pier and the winner is the one who travels furthest before crashing into the sea.

ECCENTRIC INVENTOR #2: RICHARD POCKRICH (ABOUT 1690-1759)

One handy thing about being rich is that you can spend all your money on wild schemes. And when a man named Richard Pockrich inherited lots of cash, he decided to do just that.

Richard liked to be called 'captain', even though he wasn't one. He was a bit weird. So it's no surprise that his inventions were a bit weird, too. One of them – which you may have seen – is the glass harp. This is a line of glasses containing different quantities of water, also known as singing glasses, or – maybe because it sounds so heavenly – the angelic organ.

Make your own

You can invent one yourself if you like – just run your wetted finger round the rim of a wine glass. Now, get another identical glass and put a bit of water in it – it will ring with a slightly higher note. Keep collecting glasses and putting a bit more water in each and you'll end up with a glass harp. It will sound a bit horrible at first, so you'll have to experiment with the amounts of water until it sounds like an choir of angels – or at least, not too tuneless. Glass harps even became quite popular. Even proper composers like Christoph Willibald Ritter Von Gluck (a seriously busy composer, who wrote nearly 50 operas, 8 ballets and a small pile of instrumental music, too) used them occasionally. All very nice – and isn't Willibald a great name?

Though a glass harp is possibly slightly bonkers, Richard wouldn't be in this book if that was his only invention. A much weirder scheme was his plan to make everyone's life better. Well, not everyone's. Not servants, for instance. On the contrary. His idea was to select a good healthy servant (Richard thought a 'kitchen wench' would be ideal), stick a tube into her bloodstream and pop the other end into an old posh person. This would, Richard felt sure, do the posh person no end of good and make them young and perky again. Given a sufficient number of servants, the posh person could live practically forever. (Just in case people didn't fancy draining their servants' blood, he had an alternative scheme to make them at least look young again: all they had to do was get some brown paper, soak it in vinegar and then wrap it round their wrinklier areas. After a few hours, their skin would be all smooth and lovely.) Some people do say a little bit of vinegar in water can be good for cleaning the skin, but putting the pure stuff anywhere near your eyes or nose is likely to sting...

There was just one flaw in his plan, as far as Richard was concerned, and it wasn't the fate of the servants (or the fact that it was utterly mad and would probably have killed off the people it was tried on): if ladies and gentlemen all lived for a long time, how would their deserving offspring ever get their hands on their inheritances? Where would Richard himself be if his dad had lived for thousands of years? It was just as well that he was good at brilliant schemes: he suggested the problem could be avoided very simply, by passing a law that said that 'anyone attaining the age of 999 years shall be deemed to all intents and purposes dead in law'. Once officially – though not actually – dead, their relatives would be allowed to claim their inheritances. The not-really-dead people would no doubt be a little irritated by this, but at least they would have their 1,000th birthdays to look forward to.

47

So, what would people do to enjoy their massively extended life spans? Richard had the answer: fly. He planned to provide everyone (well, again, everyone who mattered) with a pair of wings for the purpose. For those who weren't into such strenuous activities and preferred to take things easy, Richard devised some entertainment, to be provided by an orchestra composed of twenty drums, each with a different size and pitch. To avoid all the costly performers required by a usual orchestra, Richard's version needed only a single drummer, who would have all the drums arranged around him or her in a circle.

I'm sorry to have to report that Richard didn't make it to 999, or even to 99. He died at the age of about 70, in 1759. And, sadly, there seem to be no paintings of him as an old man, so there's no way to check whether his skin looked all lovely and youthful or not.

TOUGHER TEETH

The world is full of things to worry about, from missing buses to passing exams, but apparently one of the things that bothered people in 1923 was the possibility that their teeth were insufficiently exercised. Otherwise, it's hard to imagine why Mr Purdy should have come up with his teeth-exercising device. It was cunningly simple, just a plate tailor-made to fit the teeth of the user, assuming there were any – users, that is, but teeth as well, come to think of it. The plate was attached to a spring and the spring was attached to a wall. To get a really fit, muscular set of teeth, all you had to do was bite on the plate and wobble your head about a lot, pulling against the spring to give your teeth a thorough workout.

An even more cunning version of the exerciser included two plates, which were joined together by the spring. This marvellous modification allowed two people to exercise their teeth at the same time, adding to the fun as well as the health benefits. A bit like a tug of war except with a spring and teeth instead of a rope and arms.

It's possible that one reason this didn't catch on was the consequence of one of the competitors opening their mouth at the wrong moment...

LABOUR SAVERS?

Most inventions, bonkers or otherwise, are devised to save effort, which is great if the intended user is actually making any – effort, that is. But sometimes, they're just not – or they're making less than using the invention would involve. Take the spaghetti fork, invented in 1969. No, really, take it, I don't want it. It looked very much like a normal fork, just a little fatter. One can only assume that it was intended for all those people who either:

a) don't know how to pick up spaghetti with a fork
Or:
b) do know, but find it too tricky.

To use the fork, all you have to do is stick it into your spaghetti, and press in the handy plunger. This rotates the end of the fork, so the tasty pasta is coiled on to it. Brilliant. Yet pointless. Plus, it takes one hand more than the usual way of eating spaghetti.

Another 'labour saving' device is aimed at spider-rescuers. Invented in 1993, it's a tiny ladder with suction cups at the ends. If a keen spider-rescuer is equipped with one of these, and spots one of their favourite arachnids trapped in the bath, he or she doesn't have to pick it up - or, if spider-shy, coax it on to a piece of paper. Instead, he or she simply goes and fetches the ladder, sticks the ends to the top and bottom of the side of the bath, and encourages the spider towards it. Any spider with a reasonable amount of enthusiasm and agility will happily clamber up to the top. Then all that remains to be done is to move the spider from the top of the bath to the floor or garden, and remove and store away the ladder. Simple.

A 1980s invention was a bit more pricey, but – supposedly – just the ticket for all those people who hated housework but weren't prepared to wait for a household robot to be invented (see page 30). It was nothing less than an entirely self-cleaning house. Not surprisingly, its inventor, Frances Gabe, took out over 30 separate patents over a period of more than 25 years before she had it just right. To convert your own ordinary old-fashioned, clean-it-yourself house into a magical newfangled self-cleaning version, all you need to do is get your parents to have hot water sprinklers plumbed into every room, together with drainage systems and a network of hot-air blowers. Then, simply store away, remove or cover anything that isn't waterproof – books, bedding, soft furnishings, electrical items, pets, a few things like that. Best also to move any small objects that might be washed or blown away – pens, coins, iPods, that sort of stuff. Finally, evacuate the premises. 45 minutes later the interior of your house will have been efficiently cleaned and blown-dry.

Charles Babbage was a Victorian genius who built advanced mechanical calculators and designed the first computer. He also came up with some other important and significant ideas and inventions, worked out new ways to break codes, and set up the British Astronomical Society, the Society for the Advancement of Science, and the Statistical Society. He also had a few rather odd ideas. And lots that were downright bonkers...

Charles was born on Boxing Day 1791 (and so was probably cursed for the rest of his life with just one lot of presents per year). Being a rather sickly child, he was educated mainly at home, where he proved to be extremely clever, especially at mathematics. He was also into inventing things from an early age, including a device to help him walk on water ... which unfortunately didn't.

Charles was soon off to Cambridge University where, after passing his exams, he became a mathematics lecturer. From 1828 to 1839, he was the Lucasian Professor of Mathematics at Cambridge, a position only given to real clever clogs (like Isaac Newton, who worked out the maths of gravity and the laws that moving objects obey, and Stephen Hawking, who unlocked the mysteries of massively massive objects called black holes).

Charles's big project, which he started in the 1820s, was to build what we would call a computer. He started by constructing a machine that could do tricky sums, called a 'Difference Engine'. And then he built another one. Both were stuffed to bursting with wheels and cogs, and they worked just fine (you can see them at the Science Museum in London, along with half of Charles's brain).

Next, he went on to design a proper computer, called the Analytical Engine, which could be programmed using punch cards, work out sums, store the answers in its memory and print them out on big bits of paper. Charles's buddy, Ada Lovelace, wrote the programs for it all ready to feed in to it and make it do clever, computery things. Brilliant. Or at least it would have been if it had ever been built - but the craftsmen Charles employed to build it never completed the job. For many years it was thought his computer was never made because the accuracy needed to build the parts wasn't achievable at the time. However, in 1991, the Science Museum did build the Engine using Charles's plans, working to 19th-century standards, and it worked very nicely. A more likely reason the craftsmen didn't build it is that Charles could be a tiny bit annoying to work with.

Charles was a very active kind of chap, and when he wasn't fiddling with his computer, he focused his enormous brainpower on all sorts of other things, such as counting all the broken panes of glass in a factory. There were 464. He then spent ages investigating what the cause of each breakage was, and finally published his findings in 1857 as a 'Table of the Relative Frequency of the Causes of Breakage of Plate Glass Windows'. Some of the fascinating reasons for the breakages were: 'Pushing Against', 'Crowd', 'Rioters', 'Drunken men women or boys' and the highly informative 'Persons throwing various things'.

Perhaps feeling that some explanation for this project was called for, Charles wrote that his table 'will be of value in many respects, and will, we, hope induce others to furnish more extensive collections of similar and related facts'. Sadly (for Charles), no such extensive collections appeared - well, other than from Charles himself, who went on to make a list of his 165 least favourite 'street nuisances'.

Among other conceivably useful investigations, Charles tried spending some time in a drying machine, in order to ... well, just to see what would happen really. As this apparently turned out so well, he tried sitting in an oven (set to 129 °C), taking his pulse and finding out how much he sweated. A bit later, he made a trip down a volcano (Mount Vesuvius, in Italy), to see what it was like. At the time, Vesuvius was busy squirting out molten lava every few minutes. Charles carefully timed the intervals between the lava bursts, and ventured down to the lava bed in between them. He nipped off smartly just in time to escape being boiled and fried.

Charles did have rather a lot to put up with. He was an early campaigner against noise, especially that caused by street musicians, and he succeeded in getting a law passed against street noise. In response, street musicians played outside his house for hours on end.

Charles died, much to his annoyance, in 1871, too soon to get on with another of his grand schemes, which was to set up a national network of tin tubes, so that people could speak to each other over huge distances. Their conversations might have been a bit handicapped by the fact that it would have taken 17 minutes for a message to travel along his tubes from London to Liverpool (and each reply would take another 17 minutes to return). One would have to shout rather loudly too, which wouldn't do a great deal to further his anti-noise campaign.

STRANGE SPORTS

Not every invention has to be a contraption, gadget or gizmo. Some very useful inventions are ideas, or sets of rules – like democracy, football, the Eurovision song contest, or queuing. On the other hand, some idea-type inventions are bonkers. Like these strange sports...

BED RACING

A simple sport to explain, if not to see the point of, bed racing is a team game: one person lies in a bed and the others push it round a course as fast as they can. Not much more to say about that one really.

BOG SNORKELLING

At the annual world bog-snorkelling championships, which are held every August in Wales, contestants swim along a ditch cut in a bog. They may only propel themselves forwards using flippers and must breathe through a snorkel at all times.

WILL YOU STOP TRYING TO BREATHE IN FOR A MINUTE! I'M COMPLETELY STUCK!

START

BURNING BARREL ROLLING

Every year on 5th November, men, women and children carry burning barrels through the winding streets of a little town called Ottery Saint Mary. They've been doing this since the 17th century for some reason that's lost in the mists of time, but which probably wasn't a very good one in the first place. There are special small burning barrels for children, bigger ones for women, and finally seventeen huge ones for men. They're each lit outside a different pub and then carried around through the village to the town square.

CHEESE RACING

Simple to explain, but rather dangerous to play – all you do is roll a big cheese (Double Gloucester, since you ask) down a particularly steep hill (again, since you ask, in Gloucestershire), while people, frequently wearing fancy dress, try to catch up with it. The idea is to overtake the cheese if possible, but in fact the cheese nearly always wins. The winner is the first person to grab the cheese and run over the finish line.

CHESS BOXING

Punch someone a bit. Play some chess with them. Do some more punching. Bit more chess. Repeat several times. And that's chess boxing. It's actually quite popular in the USA and is starting to catch on in a small way in the UK.

EXTREME IRONING

Ironing is of course usually very dull and best left to grown-ups if at all possible. In an attempt to liven it up a bit, extreme ironing was invented in 1997. The rules are simple - you just have to iron while doing something 'extreme' - well, dangerous - like deep-sea diving, canoeing, mountaineering or waterskiing.

KABADDI

Kabaddi is a strange sport which has been around for centuries and is played in several countries, though the rules were only agreed on properly in Japan in 1979. It's played on a field, with two teams of seven players. One team links arms and a player from the other team takes a turn as a 'raider', running across to the first team and trying to prise one of the players away from the others before running back to his own team. To make it trickier, raiders have to hold their breath. As it's rather hard to be sure that someone really is holding their breath while they're running about, the raider has to shout 'kabaddi' over and over again while playing.

LAWN-MOWER RACING
This is probably the most popular weird sport there is, with several groups of lawn-mower racers around the world. The lawn mowers have to be tested first to make sure they actually do cut grass - but then the grass-cutting bits are removed and the mowers race against each other.

SHIN KICKING
Since the 17th century, people in the Cotswolds have been kicking each other and falling over a lot. All in the interest of sport, of course. The idea is simple - kick your opponent so hard they fall to the ground, at which point you get one point (though I must say I don't get the point myself). This goes on for five minutes, which is the length of one round. The winner of the round is the person with most points, and there are three rounds - whoever wins most of them wins the game. There are now annual shin kicking tournaments at something called the 'Cotswold Olympicks'. The only way players are allowed to protect themselves is to pad their shins with hay.

UNICYCLE HOCKEY

Learning to ride a bike can be quite tricky - you wobble all over the place at first. So riding a unicycle - a one-wheeled bike - must be even harder. It's hard to see why anyone would want to make things almost impossible by combining attempting to ride a unicycle with playing a sport - let's say hockey - but someone did. And the weird sport of unicycle hockey was born. In case you're wondering whether such a sport is even possible, let alone popular, you may be surprised to hear that there are actually teams in Australia, Canada, Germany, the UK and the USA. What's more, some people have even tried playing unicycle hockey on ice. Ice skating is already a tricky activity. On ice, simply not falling over is difficult - moving yourself around in a non-random, non-panicky way needs plenty of practice. So riding a unicycle on ice, while at the same time playing hockey ... well, the word 'tricky' doesn't begin to describe it.

ZORBING

Another sport with simple rules, this one needs a bit of specialist equipment in the form of two huge transparent plastic balls, one inside the other.

Up to three people get inside the balls, and strap themselves in place. Then the ball inside a ball is rolled down a hill - and that's all there is to it. In case it's not exciting enough for the participants, water can be placed in the inner ball to get them all wet.

INVENTIONS YOU CAN EAT, IF YOU'RE BRAVE

Recipes are inventions, too – someone had to invent fried fish (closely followed by chips, vinegar and – if you're that way inclined – mushy peas). Here are some less successful dishes, together with the countries they were invented in.

DOG SOUP: CHINA

SQUIRREL BRAIN SCRAMBLED WITH EGGS: USA

FRIED FRUIT BAT: SAMOA

BOILED COW'S STOMACH LINING WITH ONIONS IN WHITE SAUCE: UK

DEEP–FRIED SCORPION: LAOS

BAKED TARANTULA: VENEZUELA

GRILLED GUINEA–PIG: PERU

DONKEY STEW: FRANCE

WHAT WERE THEY THINKING?

Some inventions are just so totally doomed to failure from the start that they make you wonder whether their inventors actually knew anything about the problems they were trying to solve. Like the Scarecat, invented in 1884 in the USA by John Nelson. Inspired – if that's the word – by the idea of the scarecrow, John decided to develop something similar that rats and mice would be frightened of, which would discourage them from coming into his house at night. When I say 'develop' here, I mean, 'draw a picture of a cat with luminous paint and leave it in the kitchen'. When I say 'similar', I mean it has the word 'scare' in it, and when I say 'be frightened of', I mean 'ignore'.

Then there was the foot-hooter, designed for those occasions when it's necessary to walk in step, such as when you are a member of a team of stretcher-bearers (this was invented during the First World War, so there were plenty of such occasions). The invention was quite simple, just a set of hooters fixed to the soles of the bearers' shoes, each of which made a loud 'parp' at every step. Far from thinking that lots of parping noises might not be what you want when you're lying injured on a stretcher, the inventor suggested that, by using a set of differently pitched hooters, the stretcher-party might learn to play a little tune to entertain you.

USA TODAY

August 10th, 1904

BURIED ALIVE?

You'll be out in a jiffy if you remembered to purchase, install and get yourself interred in one of our patented devices for signalling from graves. Simply pull the cord and a flag will be raised and a bell rung up in the graveyard, attracting the attention of grave diggers, mourners and clergy alike. Fully air-conditioned for your comfort while you wait.

VICTORIANA

In the Victorian period, new technologies swept the UK and the USA, too. From railways to steam-shovels and from electric light-bulbs to vacuum cleaners, great inventions were everywhere. Perhaps it was the success of these gadgets that encouraged people to think that inventing useful stuff is easy. Here are some devices that show it isn't.

Silent alarm clock, 1882

It's obviously not very nice to be woken up by a jangling alarm clock, so this invention offered a more peaceful solution, in the form of a set of 60 corks which dropped on to the sleeper's face at getting-up time. The only disadvantages were:

1. Having to start your day by picking up 60 corks;

2. The hideous appearance of the thing;

3. Getting a mouthful of cork, should yours happen to be open and ceiling-facing.

Bath portmanteau, 1876

Portmanteaus were a popular Victorian gizmo, and not bonkers at all. They were simply big, strong, folding travel cases that the Victorians could stuff all sorts of stuff in when they went off in one of their recently invented railway trains for one of their recently invented seaside holidays. But what, wondered Ethelbert Watts, if one's train journey ended up at a hotel where no baths had yet been installed? (Plumbing was still a bit primitive in 1876, when he was doing his wondering.) How brilliant would it be if one could have a bath in one's portmanteau? Well, astonishingly brilliant of course! So he invented one, made of waterproof canvas, that unfolded into a small but fairly comfy bath. All one needed was a ready supply of hot water. All, that is, apart from somewhere to pour the water away. And a means of drying the portmanteau before repacking it again.

Breath-powered foot-warmer, 1877

Why don't people blow on their toes on cold days, like they do on their fingers? Well, a) they'd need to be pretty bendy and b) it would make them look a bit silly. But if they had purchased a Pedal Calorificator, they could have kept toasty while remaining seated – in chilly railway carriages for instance. Simply a face-mask and two tubes that went down to the inside of one's boots – very popular footwear in Victorian times, the Pedal Calorificator cunningly made use of the nicely warmed air that people breathe out, but which is usually entirely wasted. Of course, as the tubes would carry air both ways, you'd want to make sure your feet were nice and non-cheesy before use. So, the Calorificator would have dealt very nicely with a) – probably not b) though.

Horse lanterns, 1879

Despite the many new forms of transport invented in the 19th century, from penny-farthings to motor cars, horses remained popular with lots of people, and were still to be found on the road in large numbers. Some of them had to put up with daft inventions, like having lanterns stuck on their heads (rather than to the carriage they pulled, as was usual). The idea of this invention was that it would allow 'both horse and rider to see the condition of the track and the objects in it much more plainly and at a greater distance than when a lantern is placed in the carriage'. Possibly the inventor wasn't that familiar with horses, and in particular with the fact that they do move their heads up and down and from side to side quite a bit. So, a dark street containing lots of horses with lanterns on the heads would be a bit like a crowd of people randomly waving bright torches around, probably startling and annoying each other no end. In fact it would be EXACTLY like that.

Steam horse, 1878

Horses were often frightened by the new steam-trams that shared the streets with them in many 19th-century cities, but a man named Mr Mathewson thought he knew how to avoid this – by covering the front of the tram with a dummy horse. He didn't think the fact that the horse was enormous, had wheels instead of legs and had a jet of smoke emerging from its rump would disturb actual horses, or humans, for that matter, in the least.

Dishwasher, 1885

Dishwashers first started to became popular in the 1980s, yet they had been invented a century earlier. Why didn't they catch on sooner? Well, modern dishwashers work by keeping the plates in racks and squirting them with water, but the 19th century version was the opposite: to use it, one had to clamp all the dishes in place, and then rotate the lot of them through two lots of water, before unclamping them all and putting them on a rack to dry. And it was called the dishwasher for a very good reason – give it, say, a cup to wash and it just would laugh at you, as there was nowhere to clamp it. Well, it wouldn't actually laugh, but it wouldn't wash it, either.

Walking on the ceiling, 1893

You know how Spider-Man manages to walk up walls? No? Well, I don't know quite how this invention worked either, but it definitely involved a trapeze-artist. She had 'attachments to the soles of her shoes', which helped her walk upside down on a board suspended from a theatre ceiling. A report mentions that 'the performer has frequently fallen', but it does then add reassuringly 'but so far no serious accident has occurred'. So that's all right then.

Electroplated corpses , 1891

Some Victorian inventors seem to have had rather odd ideas about the sort of thing that people would actually want to use. Like Dr Varlot. His system for covering dead bodies in a layer of copper may well have worked, but what would you do with the ... er ... product? A few years later an even 'better' scheme was invented: a method of encasing dead people in blocks of solid glass. Handily – if one didn't have the space, money or inclination for the simply enormous, terribly heavily and awfully horrifying result – a head-only option was available. It could make a nice paperweight or an unusual birthday gift, I suppose.

Bonkers bikes

For some reason, Victorian inventors seem to have been obsessed with coming up with amazing bike-related inventions, including…

 The combined tricycle and printing press, which was invented in 1895. A newspaper report said:

An unusual vehicle has recently been observed in the streets of Paris: a complete, mobile printing-press! The rear wheels of the tricycle have rims to which solid rubber tyres have been secured with strong elastic bands: on its outer circumference, each tyre carries embossed printing-types enabling all sorts of short advertisements to be composed. A tank behind the driver's seat feeds the printing-ink through a tube to rubber rollers in continuous contact with the rear wheels. Between these inking-rollers a rotating fan, driven from the wheels, blows a downward stream of air on the street to free it from dust. In this way, the advertisement is printed on a clean background to make it legible for a prolonged period of time.

The Vélo-douche, a bike-powered shower – the harder you cycled, the more water the shower pumped over you. Although you'd probably get a bit sweaty in the process.

The 'Eiffel tower' bicycle, which was simply a very tall bike indeed – over three metres high in fact. Very difficult to mount, impossible to use under bridges, horrible to fall off and a nightmare to balance when stopped – but great otherwise.

ECCENTRIC INVENTOR #4:
THOMAS EDISON (1847-1931)

Thomas Edison was perhaps the most famous inventor of all, and definitely the one with most patents to his name – 1,093, to be exact. As he invented so many things, it's hardly surprising that, along with some brilliant ideas (the light bulb, for instance, or the phonograph), Thomas came up with a few oddities, such as:

A gunpowder-powered helicopter. Thomas built one of these in the 1880s. It immediately – but perhaps not altogether surprisingly – exploded. Luckily it was only a model one, but nevertheless his laboratory was never quite the same again.

A device for phoning the dead. In Thomas's time, people were excited by the idea of the telephone but not so excited by the rather rubbish sound quality of those that actually existed, so inventing new sorts of phone was very popular. But only Thomas seems to have tried to make one to phone up dead people. I say seemed because no trace of the device – if it really existed – can be found. Maybe it was 'spirited' away.

The voice-powered sewing machine. This one did work but only if the user shouted at it, loudly and a lot, so it wasn't exactly an improvement on the conventional sort.

SCIENCE COULDN'T STOP THEM

Something for nothing always sounds a great idea, and many inventors have tried to build contraptions to help them to get just that. They're called perpetual motion machines, and they're supposedly devices which go on doing their stuff - like pumping water or spinning round - forever. In some cases, the idea is that they should be able to supply useful energy to their owners at the same time.

The first such machine was designed in about 1240, by Villard de Honnecourt - a French architect. Seven heavy hammers were fixed around a wheel. The idea was that as the wheel turned, they'd swing out, so they stuck out further on one side of the wheel than the other. As a result, that side would be heavier and would sink down, and as it did the hammers would swing in again, making that part of the wheel lighter again. As a result, the wheel should turn constantly. Unfortunately, in reality both sides would be just the same weight, whatever position the hammers were in, so it wouldn't even start turning, let alone keep going.

Other inventors, like Pierre de Marcourt, thought magnetism might help. Pierre made a hollow wheel with magnets attached to the rim and another, unfixed magnet rattling round inside it. Depending which way round they are, magnets can push or pull each other, and Pierre's idea was that the magnet inside the wheel would push those on one side of it and pull at those on the other, making the wheel turn. It didn't.

Neither of these endlessly spinning wheel ideas sounded all that promising in the first place, but another magnetic gizmo sounded a bit more likely. The idea was to use a magnet to attract a metal ball, and pull it up a ramp. Just before the ball reached the magnet, it would fall through a hole and roll down a track which would deliver it to the bottom of the ramp again where it would repeat its journey. In fact, any magnet strong enough to pull the ball up the ramp would be too strong to allow it to fall through the hole, so instead the ball would just roll up the ramp and stick to the magnet.

Another apparently cool idea was a water-based device invented by the appropriately named Robert Fludd in the 1630s. His idea was to use a pump to squirt water over a water wheel, making it rotate. The water wheel could then be used to power the pump. But, as it takes more power to pump the water than the wheel could supply, the pump wouldn't actually do anything. However, a few people were still trying to get this one to work right up to the late 19th century, long after scientists had sorted out the laws of energy.

These showed that perpetual motion machines are simply impossible: energy cannot be produced or destroyed - it can only change its form.

This wasn't enough to stop some inventors though, and in 1900, the perpetual water motorcar was invented. An article published at the time explains that the water motorcar works thanks to its own weight and that of its passengers, which presses down on the containers mounted above the front and rear wheels. The containers are full of water, and pipes lead from them to the back of the vehicle. When the containers are squeezed, the pressure travels down the pipes and is directed at the back of the vehicle, hence - and here's the dodgy science - pushing the thing along. The only thing the inventor thought might be a problem was that it might work too well, going so fast that it might run people over. So the article says he '... has provided a "cow-catcher" at the front, by means of which unfortunate persons who inadvertently get in the way are to be gently waived aside'.

With a slight modification, this one could indeed have worked, but not perpetually. Nothing at all would have happened with the water containers and pipes all closed off as planned, but if big holes had been drilled at the left-hand ends of the pipes, just before they bent up towards the back of the car, the water would have squirted out behind it and perhaps pushed it forward. But the carriage would quickly have sunk as the water was squeezed out of the cylinders on to the wheels. As soon as it had reached its lowest point and the water was all gone – after a metre or so – it would have stopped, leaving a lot of stranded passengers and a very wet street.

CLEVER BEDDING

Have you ever been in that awful dilemma where you feel a bit too hot or too cold in bed and yet just don't have the energy to move the duvet? No? In that case Helmer Hedberg's gadget would be of no use to you. Helmer, a Swedish inventor, devised a complicated contraption that reacted to the sleeper's breathing. It would trigger a set of pumps and motors to flap a duvet about in time with each breath. Ideal for someone who hates to be at the wrong temperature, but who isn't disturbed by a great deal of whirring, pumping sounds – not to mention a flapping duvet and sudden blasts of air.

ECCENTRIC INVENTOR #5
NIKOLA TESLA (1856-1943)

When you switch on a light or tune in to the telly, you're benefiting from the work of Nikola Tesla, a Serbian-American inventor who developed the idea of Alternating Current (AC), a type of electricity that switches direction many times per second. AC is vital for transmitting electricity over large distances, including between power stations and homes. Tesla also invented a type of motor, called an induction motor, which works without the parts touching each other, avoiding a lot of noise, heat and wear. He also built the first underwater robot, which looked a bit like a bathtub with an aerial on top.

Although he was very clever indeed, Nikola was also a little bit strange — and fussy doesn't begin to describe him. He would only eat in restaurants that would provide him with 18 napkins, and he would only stay in hotel rooms with numbers that could be divided by three. He was also terrified of pearls. If he was around today, this wouldn't have been too much of a problem. Pearls were popular items of jewellery at the time though and not just for women, but for men too — on tie pins and cuff links, for instance, which must have made his social life very difficult. This was especially unfortunate since he loved meeting people and carrying out public demonstrations in which he liked nothing better than to make electric sparks crawl all over him. For a finale, he liked to smash up all his equipment with a sledgehammer. This may have contributed to Tesla becoming very poor. However, he always kept enough money to buy a bag of bird food, which he would feed to doves – his favourite animal.

Another of Tesla's favourite things were death-rays. Having discovered how to use AC to transmit long-distance power through wires, he wanted to find a way do the same job wirelessly. If he could manage it, it would mean he could beam power to any point on Earth – and destroy whatever was there. He claimed he'd actually managed this in his New York laboratory:

'I was experimenting with vibrations. I had one of my machines going and I wanted to see if I could get it in tune with the vibration of the building. I put it up notch after notch. There was a peculiar cracking sound.

'I asked my assistants where did the sound come from. They did not know. I put the machine up a few more notches. There was a louder cracking sound. I knew I was approaching the vibration of the steel building. I pushed the machine a little higher.

'Suddenly all the heavy machinery in the place was flying around. I grabbed a hammer and broke the machine. The building would have been down about our ears in another few minutes. Outside in the street there was pandemonium. The police and ambulances arrived. I told my assistants to say nothing. We told the police it must have been an earthquake. That's all they ever knew about it.'

All this sounds rather dubious, especially as Nikola was so cagey about the date it all happened, sometimes claiming it was in 1887, sometimes in 1888, which makes it hard to check. On the other hand, there was an earth tremor in the area on 10 August 1884, which caused walls to crack and bricks to fall, and spread over an area of 181,000 square kilometres...

The depths of fashion

No one would say that fashion has to make sense, and old fashions often look daft – just look at any photos of your parents at your age. But there are some fashions that must surely have surprised a few people at the time – the 18th-century craze for false eyebrows made of mouse skin for instance. And, while a nice white set of teeth is generally thought to look good, in the 16th century, some women decided white was terribly boring, and went in for painting them blue and other weird colours instead.

A hundred years ago, a popular new hair treatment called the perm became available, which meant that people who wanted wavy or curly hair didn't have to keep messing about with it every morning, but could have it permanently shaped as they wanted it – until it was time for a haircut, anyway. People who actually had a perm when they first became available, in the 1900s, must have been very keen indeed though. The process involved sitting with at least 12 metal curlers in their hair for six hours – and, since each curler weighed over a kilogram, the fashion victim involved must have ended up with a big strong neck as well as a nicely sculpted hairdo.

Other ideas for fashionable articles didn't catch on – and the surprise is not so much that they didn't, but that anyone would think they might. Did the relative who sent Queen Victoria a bustle that played 'God Save the Queen' when she sat down really think the Queen would like it, let alone anyone else?

I suppose Victoria could always have ordered her subjects to use musical bustles if she had been keen though, much like Elizabeth I, who passed a law that made hat-wearing compulsory on Sundays. Only children younger than eight could get out of it.

Daft fashion ideas aren't just a thing of the past, mind you. For instance, it's not often you see people whose trouser legs are different colours, and that's no doubt because they haven't purchased Alison Andrews' colourful 1999 invention: pairs of trousers which can be separated and remixed with other such trousers to create a whole range of combinations.

It'll never catch on...?

Reading through this book, you may be wondering how some inventors could have thought that their bonkers ideas would catch on. Well, maybe they were inspired by the examples of some completely pointless things which actually did rather well, like these:

Pet rocks

What makes something a good pet? Being friendly, furry, fun to be with? So, a hard, smooth and not-very-lively object like a rock is bound to lose out to a puppy or kitten – isn't it? Well, in the 1970s there really was a bit of a craze for pet rocks, and so many were sold (especially around Christmas 1975) that their inventor became a millionaire. Each came in its own box, lined with straw and supplied with air-holes. They came with training manuals, too, which explained how easy it was to teach the rocks to 'stay' and 'sit', but said that they needed a bit of help with 'roll over' and 'attack'.

Crinolines

In the early 19th century, there was a craze for wide skirts – the trendiest people got wider and wider ones until they were wider at the base than they were high. Women would wear several layers of petticoats underneath their skirts to spread them out. But as the fashion got wider still, the number of petticoats needed steadily increased, and so did the temperature of the person wearing them.

Then someone had what, presumably, seemed to be a great idea at the time – a metal cage in the shape of a dome, which was worn under the skirt. This was called a cage crinoline, and it was a real bother, however fabulous it made one's dresses look. Some crinolines were nearly two metres wide, which meant that they were forever knocking things over, frightening dogs and generally being a nuisance. Going upstairs, through doors or into carriages was usually a challenge and often nearly impossible, and sitting down was very tricky indeed.

The worst thing of all was that, if they were nudged sharply, or caught by a gust of wind, the crinolines would swing up, revealing a glimpse of the wearer's legs. This was a terribly shocking thing to happen to a young lady at the time, enough to make her come over all faint. But fainting was the very last thing she could afford to do, since, if she actually fell or lay down in the crinoline, her legs would be absolutely and thoroughly on display, in the most shocking manner imaginable. On the whole, it's rather amazing that crinolines remained the height of fashion for years.

Ice hotels

When you go on a holiday in a cold country, do you expect your room to be warm and comfortable? If you do, this Scandinavian invention isn't for you. Every winter, several ice hotels are built out of carved blocks of ice and fitted out with various bits of freezing furniture and fittings, too – even some of the drinking glasses are made of ice. The hotels are so popular that Canadian and Romanian versions have been built, and in Scandinavia itself there is even a whole village built once a year out of ice and snow.

Poison-detecting cups

In 15th and 16th century Europe, there was a great deal of arguing between powerful families, and every now and then someone would be murdered. One popular way to kill someone was by poisoning, and it's said that Lucrezia Borgia, the Pope's daughter, had a special ring with a built-in poison bottle, handy for popping into her enemies' drinks when she felt murderous. These rumours led to a certain amount of nervousness about what might be lurking in one's favourite drink, which in turn led someone to invent poison-detecting drinking glasses, designed to shatter at the presence of the merest drop of poison. When I say designed here ... well, let's just say they absolutely did not work one tiny little bit. Why no one thought to test one with some actual poison is a mystery.

Luminous sundials

Most inventors sincerely believe – or at any rate, hope – that their inventions are a great idea and just what everyone needs. But not Fred O'Brien. As a joke, he wrote to a design magazine in 1980, telling them about the wonderful luminous sundials he had invented – ideal for night-time use. The magazine loved the idea and published an article about them. Soon after, a TV company contacted Fred, asking if they could show the dials on their programmes, and a businessman even offered to produce them for him for free. Fred thought the joke had gone far enough, and pointed out that the dials did not actually tell the time – but the businessman wasn't going to let a little thing like that stop him, and arranged for pocket versions to be made by a factory in Hong King. And so, in March 1981, they were.

TV converter

In Britain, TVs first went on sale in the 1930s, but colour versions only appeared in 1967. Even then, there was only one colour channel for several years, and the sets were very expensive indeed. However, instead of buying a colour TV, you could purchase a 'converter' for your black-and-white set. This was deceptively simple – it fitted over the TV screen and was made of transparent plastic strips: green at the bottom, yellow in the middle and blue at the top. If you happened to be watching a program which was set outdoors, on a nice sunny day, on a lawn, with some … er … sand dunes in the distance, it must have been very convincing. Otherwise, it definitely wasn't. Yet a surprising number of people actually bought them.

Tamagotchis

Wouldn't it be irritating if you had a little machine that beeped at you until you pressed a button, and then did the same thing again a few minutes, or a couple of hours, later? Wouldn't it be even more annoying if you had to press several buttons, and had to make sure you pressed the right ones the correct number of times? Especially if all you got out of all this messing about were some patterns on the screen of the device – and some more beeping. Yet Tamagotchis, as such devices were called, were incredibly popular electronic 'pets' in the 1990s. Children would buy whole sets and even give them to their parents to 'feed' – or press the buttons – while they were out.

CUNNING COMBINATIONS

If you want to come up with a bonkers invention of your own, a good start is to combine two different gizmos into one amazing device. Here are some actual examples to get you started:

Lollipop / drinking straw

A lollipop with a hollow stick that went right to the top of the lickable bit, which meant that, if you stuck the other end in your favourite beverage and sucked, you could enjoy the flavour of the fruity lolly at the same time as your cola, milk or even tea.

Dog leash / umbrella

An umbrella with the handle coming out of the top of the canopy, with an attachment for a dog lead, so that you can hold it over your pet pooch to keep him or her dry.

Potato / tomato

By grafting the top of a tomato plant on to the roots of a potato, you actually can get a plant which gives you both crops. Oddly enough, Luther Burbank, its inventor, also produced plants with potato tops and tomato roots. As you might expect, these produced no crops whatsoever.

Hat / drink-can holder / megaphone/ ear trumpet

This was really a flexible cone-shaped hat with a small hole at the tip. It was patented, but never seems to have been produced – it would be difficult to make something soft enough to wear as a hat, while at the same time hard enough to magnify sounds (soft materials just soak them up), and small enough for a can to fit into snugly.

Knife / fork / spoon

Known as a splayd, sporf or spork, it was invented in the 1940s and occasionally used from then on. Unfortunately, it has to be quite blunt to avoid cutting the mouth, so it's not very useful.

Car / boat

This is known as an 'amphibious vehicle'. Various versions are used by the military, so they don't need to get out of a car or tank and into a boat when they come across a river. There are models designed for use in ordinary streets too. Great fun, though finding suitable places where they can be driven safely into water is a bit of a job, unless you have a really clever sat-nav system.

Slippers / floor-polishers

Patented in 1915, the inventor advised that the wearer should 'begin to dance, preferably such dances as require long slides, and it will be seen that the floor-polishing operation becomes a pleasure'.

Plough / gun
Invented in 1862, this was a long-barrelled gun built into the rod that connects a plough to a horse. It could be aimed by using the handles of the plough. Best to move the horse out of the way first though.

Telephone handset / dumbbell
Designed for people who want to keep fit while they work. Presumably it must also discourage the user from talking on the phone for too long...

Mug / watch
Ideal for people who want to time how long it takes them to finish their drinks, and yet are – for some reason – unwilling to glance at their wrists, this one is simply a large mug with a small digital clock on the side.

NOVELTY SAFETY CONE

Add amusement to YOUR accidents with this novelty banana-skin-shaped safety cone. Easy to use, effective and available in yellow.

THIEF-REPELLING SUITCASE

Concerned about street crime? This patented device contains three strong steel rods that spring out of your suitcase at the flick of a switch — making it, and your valuables, almost impossible to run off with.

BIRTHDAY CAKE CANDLE EXTINGUISHER

Do you know anyone who is can't be bothered to blow out their own cake candles? Then why not buy one of these simple candle extinguishers? Position the bunny-shaped device with its mouth aimed at the candles. Press its head down, and an air jet instantly blows the candles out.

SPECIAL OFFER

For a limited period only, the THIEF-REPELLING SUITCASE comes with a free thief-discouraging spiked cover for bicycle seats.

EXPLODING GOLF BALL

Take your frustrations out on your golf ball and add power to your putt at the same time, with the amazing exploding golf ball!

BURP DEODORIZER

Do you know someone who burps? Or maybe you do yourself? If so, this simple invention is a must. Containing a charcoal filter to absorb unpleasant odours, it's very easy to use: simply put it to your lips whenever you feel a burp coming on. Then just burp through it. Its pen-shaped design means you can carry it in your pocket, so it's ready for use at all times.

BACK SCRATCH T-SHIRT

Itchy back? You won't have, if you wear this great T-shirt: just pop it on and get a friend or relative to scratch you in different locations until they've hit the spot. Then, get them to read off the letter and number that defines that square on the grid, make a note of it, and next time your back itches, just direct the nearest passer-by to scratch you at that location. Scratching person not supplied.

Not what the doctor ordered

Coming up with effective medical treatments is one of the most challenging areas of science, involving many thousands of researchers all over the world, and many billions of pounds of development money each year. But before medical science was properly understood, some people thought inventing cures was really pretty simple, and they enthusiastically recommended all sorts of weird – and often unpleasant and dangerous – medicines and other treatments. Since some people do get better if they think they've been given a great medicine, even if it's actually rubbish, some of these cures may have had some effect – if anyone could bring themselves to believe they worked.

To treat malaria, for instance, eat squashed spider-webs – or if you don't fancy that, put tansy leaves in your shoes.

For warts, simply rub the wart with a piece of meat. Bury the meat and the wart will disappear as the meat rots. Alternatively, stick a pin in your wart then stick the pin in an ash tree. The tree will get the wart instead of you.

This sticking-a-pin-in-a-tree approach could also be adapted for toothache – just drive a nail into the tooth that hurts, pull it out again and stick it in the tree. No doubt that would indeed make the patient forget about their original toothache. If for some reason you don't particularly feel like trying that one, you could always hang a dead mole around your neck instead. Or, easiest of all if you have the necessary ingredient to hand, simply smell the tooth of a hanged man.

Baldness is easy to cure – just sleep with stones in your bed, and if you have colic, stand on your head for 15 minutes. A touch of lockjaw? Just boil up some crushed cockroaches and drink.

For rabies, holding a church key is just the thing. Or, if you have a goitre (a swollen throat caused by not eating the right things), then just touch the hand of that hanged man you used earlier.

Living kings and queens were even better at curing things than dead people were. For centuries it was believed that being touched by a monarch would cure a very nasty disease called scrofula.

THAT'S ALL VERY WELL, BUT HOW AM I SUPPOSED TO CURE MY SCROFULA?

99

According to some, practically anything – skin diseases of all kinds, whooping cough, rheumatism – could be cured simply by crawling through a bramble bush. Exactly what you feel like doing if you have a terrible cough, aching joints, or sensitive skin. But not to worry – if it doesn't do the sufferer any good it's no doubt highly entertaining for their friends.

With modern technology came all sorts of dodgy new cures. For victims of poisoning, for example, John Bunyan Campbell's 1898 invention was just the ticket. The idea was to plug the poisoned person into one of those newfangled electrical circuits by fixing one electrode to their neck and the other to their feet. Now for the 'science' bit – poisons come in three varieties: animal (such as snakebite), vegetable, (toadstools, for instance) or mineral (such as cyanide). So, 'logically', you just need to stick a bit of meat on your feet for animal poisons, a nice bit of fruit or veg for the vegetable type and a piece of metal for mineral poisons. Now, switch on. Sit there for three or four hours, in half hour sessions, and the poisons all comes out. Clever eh? Did it work? Not at all.

CRAZY CLOCKS

To most people, clocks are just handy gadgets for telling the time, but for others they're an excuse to come up with weird and wonderful contraptions. One such gadget, built in Prague in 1580, was a clock in the shape of a ship. It would roll up and down a table, while playing an organ and firing its guns. Its face was rather small unfortunately, so actually using it to tell the time was tricky.

Another clock, designed in 1650, would have taken a bit of installation, as part of its mechanism had to be inserted behind the walls of a room. Its clockwork system then dragged a magnet round behind the walls, which in turn dragged a metal mouse around the inside of the walls. You could tell the time by seeing where the mouse had got to. But since the magnet would collect any stray pins or needles or other bits of metal, and drag them round the room with the mouse, the novelty might have worn off quite rapidly. Another clock, built in the 18th century, was made to look like a small woodland glade. Mushrooms displayed the hours and minutes, and a peacock bowed once a day, while an owl blinked and turned its head. A circling group of grasshoppers indicated the seconds.

HOW NOT TO SAVE THE WORLD

Some inventors think big, trying to sort out the world's problems, or save it from disaster. But some of their solutions are disasters themselves.

Halting hurricanes

Over the years, people have worked hard to come up with schemes to take the 'oomph' out of hurricanes. Some of them are quite scientific, but not very practical. For instance, a 1980s scheme involved dragging icebergs around the sea to cool parts of it down, because hurricanes can only form where the sea temperature is high enough. Dragging icebergs to the right places at the right times would probably work, if enough of them could be moved around fast enough – which seems rather unlikely.

Other solutions might work but would actually do more damage than a hurricane – like pouring enormous quantities of oil over likely hurricane-spots. Some ideas are even more hopeless, such as putting rows of enormously powerful fans along endangered coastlines. Setting up and powering the fans would be enormously expensive, and they would have to generate storm-force winds themselves to stop a hurricane. As fans have to suck just as much air in from behind them as they blow out in front, the winds would probably do as much damage to the land as a hurricane.

The worst suggestion of all is the one that has been made more often than any other to the US Coast Guard: drop a nuclear warhead in the middle of the hurricane. It isn't too clear what it would do to the hurricane, but it would certainly cause more death and destruction than any hurricane on Earth. A lot more.

Making deserts bloom

More than 10% of the world's land surface is hot dry desert. Which was far too much for Arthur Pedrick's liking. So, in 1966, he came up with this brilliant scheme to do away with them. All you need are a few large tubes, each a few thousand kilometres long and three metres or so wide. Put one end of each tube in whichever desert you fancy turning into a lush green paradise. Ferry the other ends of the tubes to Antarctica, using large fleets of tugboats. Next, make your way to the top of the highest Antarctic mountain available, dragging the tubes with you, and fix them in place near the summit. Now for the fun bit. Make a very large snowball. Push it into the end of one of the tubes and gravity will do the rest: your snowball will – with a bit of luck – roll all the way down the tube to the desert, where it will melt and provide a nice big puddle. However, you won't really have time to wait for the congratulatory messages from the grateful desert dwellers, as you'll need to keep making snowballs at a rate of about 300 per minute to make any difference. You may want to ask an adult to help. And then leave them to it.

Reducing global warming

Lots of things contribute to global warming, including the long cloudy trails that planes leave behind them in the sky. These contrails, as they are called, each trap a little of the Earth's heat, making the problem of overheating slightly worse. Some scientists have come up with a scheme to avoid this. Since contrails don't form at low altitudes, all planes need to do is fly closer to the ground. But, as the air is thicker lower down, the planes would need to use more fuel to push their way through it, which would add to global warming, too – though not quite as much as the contrails, perhaps. The increased air resistance would also force the planes to fly slower, so journeys would take a lot longer, and they'd also be incredibly noisy. But still – no contrails. Good, eh?

Peacemaking

On a slightly smaller scale, one factory manager in the 1960s had a brilliant scheme to make the insides of his factories quieter. By installing lots of microphones in the noisy areas, and connecting them to loudspeakers outside the building, he hoped to 'suck' the sound out. Sadly, this would have made no difference to noise levels indoors, but the external loudspeakers would have blasted a horrible din over the surrounding area.

WEIRD WORDS

Some words, such as 'ouch' or 'the', simply evolved over time, but many others were specially invented – 'dishwasher' or 'skyscraper', for example. And some of these word inventions are rather odd, rather pointless, or a bit of both:

CLEAVE
To separate one thing into two,
or to merge things together.

CREMNOMANIA
An obsessive interest in cliffs.

DELTIOLOGY
The study of postcards.

FLIBBERTIGIBBET
A silly person.

GEPHYROPHOBIA
An uncontrollable fear of crossing bridges,
not to be confused with:

GEPHYROMANIA
An uncontrollable urge to cross bridges.

PANTOPHOBIA
A fear of everything.

PRONK
A foolish person.

PULVERATRICIOUS
Dusty.

SMACK
A group of jellyfish.

TEGESTOLOGIST
Beer-mat collector.

WYSIWYG
(Pronounced 'whizzy-wig')
This is an acronym for 'What You See Is What You Get'
– it means that when you are working with a document
on a computer, it will look exactly the same when it
prints as the version on your screen.
As it nearly always does.

BETTER THAN BEEPS?

In the 1920s, there were lots of complaints about motorcar hooters. That may be why, in 1930, Eugene Baker came up with an alternative: the 'voice pipe'. It was simply a tube which ran from the dashboard to the front of the car. The idea was that it would relay whatever you said into it to the outside world. Eugene pointed out that the voice pipe's big advantage was that while a hooter can only really say one thing – 'parp' – his invention could be used for all sorts of messages. This could be anything from a polite, 'Excuse me...' to a more forceful, 'Get out of the way!' or even, 'Vote for me!' or, 'Buy my inventions'. The big problem was that end of the horn collected all the air as the car rushed along, and blasted it into the driver's face – making it impossible to use, as well as very annoying.

BEEP! BEEP! BEEP! BEEP! BEEP! BEEP! BEEP! BEEP!

ECCENTRIC INVENTORS #6: JOHN LOGIE BAIRD (1888-1946)

John Logie Baird was a very determined chap, who worked for many years to develop and perfect his television system, and to get people to take it seriously. And, ideally, buy it. In the end, his television was rejected – because it was a mechanical system, based on spinning wheels and flickering lights, rather than an electronic one in which a beam of electrons does the trick. However, it did enjoy a brief period of success in England in the 1920s and 1930s when those few people in who did have a television all had a Baird one.

Baird first started to experiment with television systems in 1903, when he was 15. It wasn't until 1925 that he managed to organize a demonstration of his system – in Selfridges department store in London. He kept developing new systems – even 3D ones – until his death in 1946.

Some of Baird's attempts at building televisions were a bit unnerving. One early version used a dead person's eye as a camera, and another involved a rapidly spinning disc, over two metres wide, with glass lenses fastened near the outer edge – not very securely fastened, unfortunately, as they had a tendency to break loose from the disc. When that happened, Baird explained in his autobiography, they would end up 'striking the walls or roof like bombshells. The apparatus would then get out of balance and jump from one side of the lab to the other until it was stopped or the disc tore itself to pieces.'

Another system used lights that were so bright and hot, the puppet that Baird was trying to televise burst into flames. Another one used an unprotected spinning disc, which unfortunately got itself tangled in the beard of someone who was trying to watch it. Most unhappily, this someone was a member of the Royal Society, who'd been especially invited to the first scientific demonstration of the system. Baird had really hoped to impress him.

It's just as well that Baird had a few other inventions up his sleeve – or it would have been, if they'd been any good. They included:

• An electrical device to make diamonds from coal. Baird tested this when he worked at the Glasgow Electricity company. Immediately after his experiment started, half the city was blacked out by a power cut. Immediately after that, he started looking for another job.

• Baird undersocks. Supposed to keep feet dry, these were ordinary socks impregnated with moisture-absorbing powder. They probably worked a little bit, until anyone tried to wash them, at which point the powder washed away.

• Fruit-and-insect jam. The insects weren't actually supposed to take part in the preparation, but, as John made his jam in a jungle in Trinidad, he found it impossible to avoid them.

• Pneumatic shoes — which were ordinary (though rather huge) shoes with balloons in them, for comfort. They burst on the first outing, turning out to be not very comforting at all.

• Rustless razors. Which indeed, did not rust, but instead gave the user nasty cuts, as they were made of sharpened glass.

113

Inventive instruments

There are about 20 different musical instruments in a typical orchestra, which should be quite enough for any piece of music. However, that hasn't stop enterprising inventors from coming up with plenty more, such as:

Anvil

Anvils were invented for blacksmiths to bash pieces of hot metal around on, so that the metal could be shaped into horseshoes, bits of armour, tools and many other things. They were well designed for all those jobs – but not really ideal to play tunes on. But that didn't stop various 19th century composers from writing music for them, including Richard Wagner and Giuseppe Verdi.

Laser harp

A laser harp is made of several beams of laser light, each of which is linked to an electronic device called an oscillator. When the light beams are interrupted or otherwise messed about with (by the performer's hands for instance), the notes made by the oscillator change ... a task which could be accomplished much more simply by plucking a few strings.

Porcelain piano

Built in 2008, this piano is made almost entirely of – you guessed it – porcelain. Blue and white porcelain in fact, so it looks rather like a huge, weird version of the sort of teapot your granny might have.

Prepared piano

You can make one of these yourself, just by putting a few odds and ends on to the strings of an ordinary piano – like nuts, bolts or paperclips. Then just play the piano as normal. Sounds weird in more ways than one, but pieces of music really were written for prepared pianos by the American composer John Cage in the 1960s. If you do try this yourself, you'd best unprepare it again afterwards, before anyone notices.

Saw

If violinists ever get sick of their usual instruments, they can always use saws instead. To play a saw, you just need to bend it into a curve, and then play it like a violin, by drawing a bow across it. Bending and flexing the saw in different ways produces different notes – all of which are rather weird and waily. Since bending a saw isn't the safest thing to do, special toothless versions are made for musical performance.

Sea organ

The sea organ is a set of 35 organ pipes built in 2005 under a concrete platform on the coast at Zadar, Croatia. It is 70 metres long, and the pipes make musical sounds when the sea or wind moves across them, which is all the time. It sounds very nice, apparently.

72 string guitar

One simple way of coming up with a weird invention is to make an unnecessarily large version of something more normal – like a guitar. A Japanese artist called Yoshihiko Satoh built just such an instrument in 2007, by making a guitar with 12 necks, each of which has six strings. Why? I don't know.

Stalactite organ

Stalactites are icicle-shaped pieces of stone, produced in some caves over many centuries by slowly dripping water. In 1954, Leland Sprinkle, an American mathematician, decided that they would be ideal for music-making. So, in the Luray Caverns in Virginia, USA, he installed several dozen electrically powered rubber mallets. At the press of a button, a mallet strikes its stalactite, which makes a ringing sound. The buttons are grouped together to make a keyboard which can be used to play pieces of music on the 'stalacpipe' organ, which is the largest musical instrument in the world, and still in use today.

Theremin

The Theremin is an electronic instrument invented by a Russian man by the name of Theremin. It uses devices called oscillators, which use a changing flow of electricity to make pieces of metal wobble quickly from side to side. The wobbles travel through the air as musical notes. Like the laser harp, the Theremin is played by the musician's movement. If you wave your arms around – or your legs, if you prefer – the Theremin detects the movement, and the notes made by the oscillators change in response. It became quite popular in the late 1960s after the astronaut Neil Armstrong – the first man on the Moon – said how cool it was.

Tiny tunes

Musical instruments have been carefully designed and developed – for centuries, sometimes – to fit the dimensions of suitable bits of body. So, piano keys are about a finger-width across, cellos are just right for cellists to hold, harps are as wide as a harpist can easily stretch, and so on. Bearing this in mind, the idea of making tiny instruments seems a little pointless, but pointlessness isn't enough to put off really keen inventors.

At just over 4 cm long, the world's smallest violin, which was made in 1973, is fairly easy to make a noise with, but almost impossible to play a tune on. The World's Smallest Grand Piano, on the other hand, can't really be played at all, as each of its keys is only four millimetres wide, so even the littlest little finger will hit several at once. Luckily it comes with a clever system that means it can play tunes all by itself, like an iPod but much more expensive.

World's smallest violin

Until fairly recently, even the tiniest instruments were at least a few centimetres wide, but now that it's possible to move individual atoms around, mini music has entered a new realm of tininess. The NanoHarp, for instance, has strings just a few millionths of a millimetre long, and each one is only about 150 atoms wide. It does actually play tunes, but the pitches are so high and the sounds are so quiet that no human – or any other living thing – can hear them. Impressive, and yet bonkers at the same time.

SNORE-STOPPERS

There are lots of ways, these days, to stop snoring, from surgery to inhalers to sticky things that hold your nostrils open and make you look silly. Most work quite well, too, but none of them were available in 1931, prompting George Rundle to come up with a whole range of snore-stopping systems. The mildest one rang a bell when the snoring started, but more advanced versions gave the snorer an electric shock, or even stabbed him or her in the arm with a pin. Yet another picked up the sounds of the snores and played them back to the snorer. Since snorers usually aren't disturbed by their own snoring, it was necessary to play back the snores very loudly. Any other sounds made by the sleeper would have been played back extra-loudly too – such as any shouts or screams caused by the startling effect of the snore-stopper. Although perhaps not likely to catch on with snorers, you can imagine this sort of thing might be quite entertaining to other people.

Dangerous devices

Most bonkers inventions are simply ... er ... bonkers – but some are deadly. Oddly enough, sometimes those are the very ones that people like.

Possets

Possets were pottery or china containers, which were given to people with coughs, colds and assorted sniffles in the 17th and 18th centuries. They were filled with warm mixtures of things like sugar, lemon juice, spices and brandy, which were very tasty and comforting. Unfortunately, they were even more popular with germs than people and, since they were sealed at the top and impossible to wash properly, they probably polished off a lot of people who would otherwise have been just fine.

Platform shoes

I'm very sorry if any of your relatives used to think these were cool in the 1970s (or maybe even still do), but sticking huge lumps of plastic or wood on your feet and wobbling around in them isn't really that good for your ankles, unless you want twisted, sprained or broken ones. And do they look super-stylish? Not really, no.

AutoVision

Television-watching while driving is not recommended by anyone, yet AutoVision – a system which projects a TV programme on to a screen in a car – makes this dangerous pursuit possible. Surprisingly, the use of AutoVision is permitted, at least in the state of Michigan, USA.

CFCs

CFCs – or chlorofluorocarbons to give them their full name – are a great idea for making fridges work really well. But they are not so good for the ozone layer, which protects the planet from the more deadly of the Sun's rays. In the late 20th century, CFCs made an enormous hole in this layer. Fortunately the hole is on the mend, now that such chemicals have been banned.

Radioactive allsorts

When Marie and Pierre Curie discovered radium in 1898, it seemed almost magical. Glowing an eerie blue-green in the dark, never growing cold and changing colour rapidly, it was one of the first radioactive elements to be isolated. When the idea got around that it could cure various illnesses, there was a radium craze. It was used as an ingredient in all sorts of things — very bad news indeed since, far from being a miracle cure, radium is deadly. It's probably the cause of the illness that killed Marie Curie. In fact, her notebooks are still so radioactive that anyone who touches them must first sign a form to say they understand the risk. Yet, for over 40 years it was added to a wide range of products, as were other radioactive materials. Products like...

Tho-Radia Face Cream

Supposedly providing instantly beautiful skin, Tho-Radia was popular in France in the early 1930s. Adverts for it claimed that it was invented by 'Dr Alfred Curie' — even though there was no such person.

Luminous watch dials

Many of the watches and lots of the clocks produced in the 1900s had numerals and hands painted with pigments containing radium, so that people could tell the time at night. The workers who painted the dials used to lick the brushes to make them the correct pointed shape, and many of them died as a result.

Radium bread

In what is now the Czech Republic, loaves of bread were made by the Hippman-Blach bakery using radium 'rich' — or, as we would now put it, 'contaminated' — water.

Radioactive toy set

By 1951, the dangers of radioactivity were well proven and quite well-known — so it's amazing that The Atomic Energy Lab went on sale that year. It was a toy that contained actual pieces of radioactive material — and it was still available in 1978!

Radioactive drinking water

Radon is a naturally radioactive gas produced by granite rocks. In the 1900s, special radon jars called Revigators were made — any water added to them would become slightly radioactive and, according to the adverts, would provide 'nature's way to health'.

Radium toothpaste

In the Second World War, a Berlin company started to produce radioactive toothpaste. Why? Because, according to the packet, 'radioactive radiation increases the defences of teeth and gums ... it gently polishes the dental enamel and turns it white and shiny.'

MAKE YOUR OWN TIME MACHINE

A lot of people think time machines, being logically impossible, are simply bonkers and will never get off the ground. Where would you be, for instance, if you went back in time and accidentally killed your ancestors? Other scientists, meanwhile, have investigated the fiendishly complicated physics involved and have concluded that, in theory, it just might be possible to build a time machine.

This is how it's done:

1. FIND A WORMHOLE

Albert Einstein showed that space and time are linked together, and that they are 'shaped' by heavy objects like the Earth and Sun. Imagine the space and time where the Solar System is located is shaped like a range of mountains. If you flew a rocket from one planet to another, it would take ages because you'd have to follow this mountainous landscape. But what if you could find a tunnel that cut straight through the mountains? It would make your journey much quicker. Einstein's theories showed that there really might be tunnels through space and time. These tunnels are called wormholes, and they could be short cuts through space. Not only that, but because space and time are linked together, you could travel to a different time, too. All very encouraging for the budding cosmic engineer, except no one has ever found a wormhole. Fear not: there's a theory that suggests that tiny little ones might pop in and out of existence all over the place, all the time. If you could find one of these, the next thing on your 'to do' list is:

2. GROW YOUR WORMHOLE

Now you need to obtain some exotic matter. There are several sorts, and the one you will need has negative mass. Mass is the amount of matter something has and negative mass is repelled by gravity, normal mass is attracted to it. No one is sure whether negative mass really exists, but, if you manage to find some, carefully introduce it to the wormhole, which will start to grow larger in response. Make the wormhole big enough to accommodate a small spaceship, then stop. As you'll be using several space vehicles, it would be simplest to do this in orbit – perhaps on the International Space Station. Actually, you might as well stay there while you:

3. STABILIZE YOUR WORMHOLE

This is – relatively – easy and absolutely necessary: if you stepped inside your wormhole now, it would collapse all over you, either crushing you, or shredding you, or both. Most annoying. Luckily, all you need to prop it open is some more exotic matter, so we can move on to the next step.

4. STRETCH YOUR WORMHOLE

Now you need another spacecraft. A nice powerful robotic one would be perfect. Position one end of your wormhole inside it, and send it off into space. You'll need to bring it home again later, so put it in orbit round the Sun or something, just so you know where it is. What matters here is getting the end of the wormhole moving: as soon as it does, the time on it will change. Einstein showed that if you can get something to move at an incredibly high speed, time (according to that fast-moving thing) will speed up, and move into the future. You could check this by taking two clocks and putting one on each end of the wormhole. They will gradually get out of step. The next bit is easy:

5. WAIT

How long you need to do this for depends on how fast your spaceship can go. Travelling at the speed of light itself is impossible, but, if you have plenty of power on hand, you might get the spaceship to go at a good fraction (say, 99.999%) of lightspeed. In that case, waiting a year should do very nicely. By that time, time on board should have moved far into the future. So, let's assume that, according to the ship and the wormhole-end it carries, the date is now AD 3000. It's time to...

6. BRING HOME YOUR WORMHOLE

Guide the robotic spaceship home, and put the end of the wormhole that was inside it next to the other end, which has been at home all this time. And that's it – you're all set to...

7. TRAVEL IN TIME

Get into your spaceship and pilot it carefully into the stay-at-home end of the wormhole, down the hole, and out at the other end. The date will now be AD 3000, so go out and enjoy the amazing end-of-millennium parties. Then, you can either return to the present by travelling the other way down the wormhole, or repeat your journey as many times as you like, moving thousands of years into the future on each trip.

The only disadvantage of this time machine is that you can't use it to travel backward in time to any point before it was built. This is because moving at high speed can only move the end of the wormhole into the future, not the past. However, it's just possible that there might be natural ways for wormholes to stabilize themselves – or at least there were when the Universe was busily forming. It's also possible that these ancient wormholes grew in size as the Universe expanded. If they did, and you could find one, then you could travel back down it to the beginning of the Universe, or just afterwards.

CINEMATIC CONTRAPTIONS

William Castle, an American film-producer, director and occasional actor, made some scary films in his time, but somehow they were never quite scary enough to satisfy him – so he started to add a few extras to their screenings, in the form of a whole series of weird inventions, many with technological-sounding names to make them seem more impressive. 'Emergo', for instance, was invented for one of his most famous films, *House on Haunted Hill*, which was made in 1959. Emergo was actually just a glow-in-the-dark skeleton, which was dangled over the audience near the end of the film, carefully timed to appear at the same time as an animated skeleton in the film. Sadly for William, the audiences weren't always very impressed and Emergo soon became a popular target for popcorn and apple-cores.

A more effective trick was 'Percepto', which was invented for a film called *The Tingler*. The film has a great idea for a monster – a centipede-like creature that lives in people's spines and can only be destroyed by screaming. Percepto consisted of a set of vibrating buzzers, which were attached to the undersides of some of the seats in the audience. They were switched on to coincide with the moment in the story when the Tingler escapes from a film into the audience, making them think it was attacking them.

'Illusion-O' (William had clearly run out of good names for his inventions by this point) was two strips of plastic – one blue-tinted and one red-tinted. When the film, *13 Ghosts*, was screened, the ghosts were all printed in red on the film print, so if an audience member was too scared to cope with them, he or she could simply look through the blue strip and they would disappear. Those made from sterner stuff could look through the red strip to see the ghosts clearly. If neither strip was used, the ghosts could be seen faintly.

USELESS UNITS

Sometimes even the most dedicated scientists get bored of the serious business of pushing back the boundaries of knowledge, and when they do, some of them invent new units of measurement, to go along with the more everyday metres, seconds and kilograms we all know and love. Here are some of the wackier ones.

In the 1940s, scientists were trying to fire minuscule bits of matter called particles at the nuclei, or cores, of atoms, and didn't always have much success. So they decided to measure the area they were attempting to hit in units called BARNS, apparently from the idea that they - or their colleagues - 'couldn't hit a barn-door with a banjo'. A barn is a trillionth of a trillionth of a square centimetre, which is about the area of a large atomic nucleus.

Encouraged by all the fun they had with that unit, they came up with a SHED, which is of course like a barn, but smaller. Actually, the shed is such a tiny unit - there are a trillion trillion sheds in a barn - that no one ever seems actually to have used it.

Then there's the CROCODILE. To most of us, it's simply a water-loving grey-green reptile with rather a lot of teeth and a tendency to bite your leg off. But to nuclear physicists - who are obviously into this whole weird-names thing - it's the name for a million volts. They might have come up with the idea because they use crocodile clips, which look a bit like crocodiles, to connect electrical equipment together. Or maybe it was deadliness of the thing that they had in mind.

The storage capacity of a computer can be measured in BYTES, MEGABYTES or GIGABYTES - a megabyte is a million bytes and a gigabyte is a billion bytes. But one byte is 8 bits, and half a byte is ... wait for it ... a NIBBLE. Geddit?

Other rather weird unitary inventions - none of which really caught on, sadly - include:

THE GLUG:
a suggested
unit of mass.

THE SLUG:
another suggested
unit of mass.

THE MUG:
yet another
one.

Everyone seems to have got bored with inventing units of mass ending in 'ug' at this point, so they turned to angles and decided to try:

THE GON:
one-hundredth of a right-angle,
or 0.9 degrees.

Then, for a new unit of temperature, someone suggested the INFERNO - a unit designed to describe how hot the core of a star is. The Sun's core is about one-hundredth of an inferno.

Closer to home, there is the NOGGIN, which is a quarter of a pint.

One unit that did catch on in a big way for many centuries - in England at least - was the PERCH. Not a particularly odd name, but the same can't be said of its definition:

THE TOTAL LENGTH OF THE LEFT FEET OF THE FIRST SIXTEEN MEN TO LEAVE CHURCH ON A SUNDAY MORNING.

NONSENSE AHEAD

Kings and queens have got a lot to answer for: for example, the invention of the ridiculous wig. When Queen Elizabeth I was getting on a bit, she had one made to cover her rapidly thinning white hair. For some reason she went for a startlingly bright red (and this was several centuries before Ronald McDonald, so she didn't get the idea from him). Then, a bit later on, King Louis XIII of France and Charles II of England both went in for much longer wigs, though fortunately rather more plainly coloured ones. As a result of all this royal popularity, wigs caught on in a big way, and before long, men and women with a bit of cash and a desire to look cool (and ideally a little bit royal) were chopping off their hair and putting wigs on instead. Sometimes the wigs were made of their own hair which seems a bit pointless, especially as they were terribly hot and itchy.

But it was Marie Antoinette, wife of the King Louis XVI of France, who really started the craze for truly bonkers hairpieces. Thanks to her encouragement, taller and taller wigs were invented, with more and more additions, like jewellery and feathers, and pieces of cloth and netting with pictures on them. The posher you were, the more ridiculous stuff you had to have on your head. One French duchess's hairdo, which she showed off at the opera in 1776, included a picture of her son, his nurse, another little boy, and a parrot. What made that one extra special was that it was constructed with hair from the heads of three genuine dukes.

No one bothered much about washing their hair, or their wigs, either, so both were very popular with lice, nits, fleas and other small pests. It's even said that mice occasionally took up residence there, too.

In 1778, rich French women who were especially patriotic as well as fashionable turned up at parties with model ships in their wigs – some of which had no fewer than 26 little guns on board. The point – if there was one at all – was to celebrate a recent naval victory over the British.

Fortunately, by the 19th century, wig fashions were in retreat, and now bonkers wigs are found only on ageing film stars and high-court judges.

BITS OF LUCK

Most of the inventions in this book were only regarded as good ideas by their inventors, although some of them did catch on a bit. Occasionally though, an inventor comes up with something quite by accident, which turns out to be just what everyone needs, even though they hadn't realized it. This process of inventing things through happy accidents is known as serendipity, and it's a nice surprise for all concerned.

Sometimes, these handy inventions are developed when people are trying to come up with something rather different. For instance, Dr Kellogg thought he'd try to make dough out of some stale cooked wheat, rather than throw it away, but instead he ended up with little flakes, which turned out to be rather yummy when toasted. What were they? The clue's in his name.

Then there was Spencer Silver, an industrial chemist whose attempt to make a super-strong glue was utterly rubbish. It resulted in a glue so weak that bits of paper could be pulled apart again easily. Ta-da – the Post-it note was born!

Another Spencer, Percy this time, was experimenting with radar systems in the 1940s when he noticed that a chocolate bar in his pocket had suddenly melted. Showing himself to be a true scientist, Percy was more interested than irritated. He decided that the very short radio-waves - now called microwaves - produced by his system might be responsible, so he rushed off to do some experiments straight away. First, he placed some corn kernels close to his experimental system, which resulted in the world's first microwave popcorn. Next he tried an egg, which exploded very nicely. (Don't try microwaving an egg yourself by the way. No, you really shouldn't - it's very messy.) As a result, Percy helped develop the first microwave ovens. Actually, he was lucky in more ways than one - he must have exposed his body to some very nasty microwaves during his experiments, and it's amazing they didn't do him harm or at least bake a few of his organs.

Another scientist with an eye for a lucky accident was a French chemist called Edouard Benedictus. In 1903, he dropped a glass flask in which he'd been doing a spot of chemistry. It shattered, but weirdly, the shattered bits all stayed together. He discovered that this was because the chemical he'd made in the glass, a plastic called cellulose nitrate, had become solid and was holding the fragments together. Edouard went on to develop a glass/plastic sandwich and it was soon used to make safety glass, which in turn was used to make car windscreens. Laminated glass like this is still often used to make all sorts of vehicle windows, bus shelters and many other things.

RIDICULOUS ROBOTS

Robots are very useful things - great at making cars, exploring space and investigating the ocean floor. Some of them, that is. Others don't seem quite as useful, though I'm sure their inventors love them just the same.

Many robots don't have the ability to move around, and those that do generally roll about on wheels. There are a few robots that can actually walk and some robots that are invented just to test out different types of new technology, such as robot limbs designed to move like animal arms and legs. Just walking isn't enough for the Robonova-1 though - not only can it climb ropes, it can swing from one branch to another too, a bit like a metal monkey. Cool to watch, but not really much use.

Some robots have even been invented just to play games - perfect if you no friends are about to play with. And, if table football is your thing, you don't need to worry if you've got no friends - several research teams around the world have developed robots to play it. It's a good way to design better robots, because table football needs fast reactions and accurate movements, but doesn't need a great deal of space to play.

There are lots of ways to deal with a Rubik's cube. You could look up the best technique on the internet, get a book full of tips on how to complete it, sit playing with the thing for days on end, or - a personal favourite - peel off the coloured squares and stick them back on in the winning pattern. Of course, you could build a robot to do it for you. There are actually several robots like this, including 'Cubot' and 'Cubestormer'. Cubestormer has four hands and can solve a cube in under 12 seconds.

Like the Rubik's cube, video games are really intended to be played by people. There doesn't seem much point in a video game that people don't play, any more than there's a point to a sock without a foot. Nevertheless, a robot called Cythbot exists, and there's just one thing it's good at: playing a video game called Guitar Hero. In the game, you - or in this case it - have to strum along on an electric-guitar-like console, following the notes that unroll on the screen before you. Cythbot does this really well. What for? I don't know.

On TV, robots tend to be quite menacing, but in the real world they're usually not scary at all. Except for the Kabutom RX-03. Designed to look like a monstrous beetle, it's a robot vehicle that weighs 15 tons and can carry up to six people inside. Sitting inside it is probably the best place to be. It looks like an enormous insect, is over ten metres long, and moves by dragging itself along on wheels using its enormous clawed legs. Terrifying.

Pointless robotic inventions aren't all that new - in 1964, a robot was developed to answer the phone. It had three little oddities:

1. It was human-sized and human-shaped – yet all it did was lift a telephone receiver, which a little rod or lever would have done just as well.

2. Once it had picked the receiver up, it couldn't actually answer the call as it wasn't equipped with a voice.

3. It looked absolutely terrifying.

Floor-cleaning robots are undoubtedly very useful. It's also nice to be able to project your favourite DVDs on to a handy screen. Combining both functions in one machine doesn't seem terribly handy, but if it strikes you as a useful idea, then you can nip out and buy a Japanese robot called the RIDC-01. As DVD projectors and floor-cleaning robots each cost a few £100 or so, you might think RIDC-01 would be fairly cheap. It actually costs over $85,000.

The whole point of robots is to do things that are useful, but that people don't want to do themselves, like putting out dangerous fires or mowing the lawn. A rather less useful robotic skill is the ability to poo. But that's what

Ecobot III does. Instead of using boring old batteries, it gets its power by digesting sewage water and then ... er ... getting rid of the leftovers about 24 hours later. Marvellous. Sadly it doesn't know how to use the toilet. Ecobot III is also known as BREADbot, which stands for Bio-Regulation and Energy-Autonomy with Digestion.

A more obviously useful machine is a robot called Waseda Okino Jaws. Sometimes, people who've had operations on their mouths or who suffer from diseases that make it difficult for them to control their muscles need to be trained to use their jaws properly again. They need to practise several times a day, so it's not always easy to have a therapist there to help out every time. Instead, Waseda Okino Jaws can be delivered to their homes, ready programmed to demonstrate the right chewing motions – the people can then copy its movements to learn how to chew properly. It all sounds like a good idea until you actually see the robot, which is a real human skull that chews and moves its jaws in every imaginable way. Handy, maybe ... scary, definitely.

That's not as scary as SlugBot, though - at least not if you're a slug. SlugBot prowls around gardens, tracking down slugs by using its advanced vision system, which recognizes their distinctive shapes and temperatures. Once it has found them, it scoops them up and puts them in a box where they die and rot. The smelly gases they produce as they decay are then burnt to provide SlugBot with power.

FAME AT LAST

There have been some great scientific breakthroughs in the last hundred years or so. Every year, the very best are rewarded by a set of international awards, called Nobel Prizes. They're handed out in a plush ceremony in Sweden, together with prizes for non-scientific things such as literature. Winning a Nobel Prize is the crowning moment of a career.

Meanwhile, there have also been some absolutely useless discoveries, many in the form of pointless inventions, and the people who come up with them have no hope whatsoever of a Nobel Prize. They do, however, have the chance of getting the opposite: an 'Ig Nobel' prize. Like their more famous namesakes, Ig Nobel prizes are awarded every year, though in the USA rather than Sweden. Here are some of the most-curious invention-related prizes that have been awarded:

ENGINEERING: a remote-controlled mini helicopter to collect snot from whales. (USA/UK)

NUTRITION: a machine to change the sound made by crunching a crisp, so the person eating it thinks it is crispier than it actually is. (Italy/UK)

NUTRITION: a bottomless bowl of soup. The point of which was to investigate whether people eat until a) they are no longer hungry, or b) there's no more food – assuming they don't actually explode, of course. And the answer is: b. (USA)

ECONOMICS: an alarm clock that runs away and hides. This was given an economics prize because it's meant to make absolutely sure that people get out of bed, so they're more likely to get to work on time. (USA)

PEACE: a cunning computer program called Bow-Lingual that translates dog barks into human language and vice versa. (Japan)

COMPUTER SCIENCE: a computer program called PawSense that can work out whether a cat is walking across your keyboard. (USA)

BIOLOGY: a non-hot chilli pepper. (USA)

REALLY BAD INVENTIONS

Some bonkers inventions are weird or pointless – but others are just plain BAD. Like these:

BAD FOR DOGS: Dog-turbine (1859)
Dexter C. Slater's invention was a disc hooked up to a gear system that provided power to run various bits of machinery. To use it, all you needed was a very patient and obedient dog to keep walking on the disc, pushing it round as it did so.

BAD FOR BACKS: Travel hammock (1889)
Mr Small's travel hammock was intended to be hung between the rows of seats on a train, for sleepy commuters on long journeys. But, as rows of train seats are really rather close together, it must have been almost equally awkward and uncomfortable to get in to, sleep in, and get out of.

BAD FIRST THING IN THE MORNING #1:
Alarm bed (1900)
A genuinely alarming bed, Ludwig Ederer's invention simply tipped its occupants to a 45 degree angle when it went off. So anyone sleeping near the edge of their bed was likely to wake up on the floor – fully awake, certainly, but also rather battered.

BAD FOR LOOKING COOL: Golf training-device (1916)
In golf, accurate and powerful swings are vital in getting the ball to go where you want it to, and to achieve such swings, posture is very important. For those who struggle to achieve correct golfing posture themselves, Hugh Rhind invented the golf training-device. Once well strapped into it, the not-so-brilliant golfer would be held in just the right position – just right for all your competitors to laugh at.

BAD FOR SURVIVAL: Spherical lifeboat (1918)
The clue to the trouble with this one is in the name. Mr Salari's lifeboat was covered in springs, so that it would bounce off anything it banged into, which might have been a reasonable idea. Making it spherical on the other hand meant that, even in fairly calm seas, it would constantly roll over and over, and so would anyone unfortunate enough to be inside it.

BAD FIRST THING IN THE MORNING #2: Silent alarm clock (1919)
This invention is certainly pretty quiet, but the sleeper might not have been when he or she wakes, since it worked by banging them on the head at getting-up time.

BAD FOR ANKLES: Spring shoes (1920)
Shoes with springs under them. I mean, it's just asking for trouble really, isn't it?

BAD FOR BABIES #1: Baby holder (1937)
The baby holder was specifically designed for all those caring 1930s parents who wished to combine looking after their delicate bundles of joy with a bit of ice skating. The inventor, Jack Milford, was an ice-hockey player and obviously didn't want his child to miss out on skating, just because it couldn't walk yet.

BAD FOR BABIES #2: Baby cage (1937)

1937 was a bad year if you were a baby. In the 1930s in London, just like today, many people rented flats to live in. Rather less like today though, those tenants with babies who lived on upper floors were encouraged to purchase special cages to put them in. Simply fix them to the outside of the flat, pop your baby in and there you go. Peace and quiet for you, and fresh air for the baby. All fine if the cage is securely attached, it's not windy, cold, hot or rainy and the baby doesn't mind heights and doesn't throw up through the sides.

BAD FOR ROAD SAFETY: Illuminated tyres (1961)

Why have a set of tyres that light up? Well, according to the advert, if you were a lady you could adjust your stockings by the roadside at night – so presumably they could also be handy if you wanted to tie your shoelaces or perhaps do a spot of reading. Which is just what you shouldn't be doing by a busy road.

Useless kitchen gadgets

Of all the rooms in the house, the kitchen is the one in which you're most likely to find a stock of useless inventions. Such as:

Electric pizza-cutter

Cutting a pizza isn't very difficult, especially if you use one of those handy gadgets with a sharp metal disc to do the job. So, why anyone would want to construct an electric version – with all the extra weight, and the need to replace the batteries – is really rather weird.

Apple peeler and corer

There are already very nice, easy to use, apple corers and peelers on the market. So the need for a special device into which an apple must first be clipped, and then rotated against a knife to remove the peel, and then unclipped, escapes me.

Milk carton holder

Milk and juice boxes can occasionally be slightly tricky to open, but once that task is out of the way they're no more challenging to pick up and pour from than a teapot. However, the inventor of the milk carton holder – a squarish plastic framework with a handle – obviously thought differently.

Tea bag holder

A special sort of clamp with which to grab tea bags and remove them from your cup when your tea is strong enough for you. Obviously invented by someone who hadn't heard of spoons.

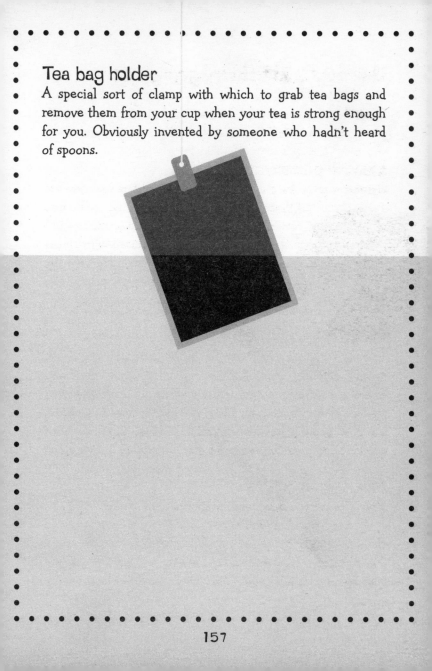

Plug mug

Strictly for people who are very protective about their favourite mug, or perhaps very worried about other people's germs or something, the idea of the plug mug is that when you need to leave it unattended for a while, you remove a special plug from it and take it away with you – so that anyone who pours a drink into it will find it all pouring out again, from the hole the plug is no longer filling. Instead of purchasing such a thing, which could be very dangerous if the plug popped out as the mug was on its way to your mouth, you could always just carry your prized mug with you wherever you go. Assuming you don't mind people looking at you oddly when you turn up with it at the swimming pool.

Chocolate fountain

This machine, once loaded with special chocolate, first melts it and then pumps it slowly up through a tube which overflows to make a gooey fountain. You can then dip strawberries or marshmallows in it to smother them with chocolate. Apart from the fact that the special chocolate that these fountains use isn't very nice, cleaning the thing would be a nightmare. Much better just to eat some yummy chocolate instead.

159

ROCKING TECHNOLOGY

Until the 20th century, one challenge that faced many inventors, sensible as well as daft, was finding a source of power. Even when domestic electric light became fairly common in the 1920s, there were often no accompanying power sockets and so some gadgets – such as early electric irons – had to be fitted into light-bulb holders. But, as far as some inventors were concerned, there was no need for any sort of electricity when there was a rocking chair to be had...

With one 19th-century invention, the power of the person rocking backwards and forwards was even used to clean the house. A large pair of bellows under the seat was connected by a tube to the sucking end of a vacuum cleaner. So, while one person rocked, another could give the room a bit of a clean. Unfortunately, the rocker didn't just have to rock, they also had to cart the chair from room to room – not to mention up and down stairs – to vacuum the whole house. Not very relaxing really, and not exactly labour-saving.

Nor was the patented butter-making chair, which was a rocking-chair with a heavy, milk-filled churn clamped to its side. Rocking the chair swished the milk about, eventually turning it into butter.

If you really wanted to use your rocking chair for housework and making dairy produce, you might want to get hold of Charles Singer's 1869 invention, too. It was another bellows-and-air-pipe arrangement, which meant that every time the chair was rocked, a blast of cool air would be directed into your face. Or, if your rocking-chair activities had left you really hot and sweaty, Richard Straube's 1899 device would have been ideal – a combined rocking chair and bath.

PERILOUS POGOS

Pogo sticks aren't the most exciting way to travel, but they would be if Gordon Spitzmesser had made anything of his 1958 gas-powered version. The idea was that every bounce would set off a small explosion inside the stick, generating tremendously high jumps and a great deal of banging. Perhaps the slight dangers involved were a factor in it not being in the shops for Christmas. Ever.

IF YOU WANT TO GET AHEAD, GET A HAT. WITH A FAN IN IT.

In 1912, there was a new problem for posh women: headaches caused – so a few people believed – by the hats they wore. The theory was that hats prevented air circulating around the head. Why the lack of air circulating round other bits of the body didn't cause their own corresponding aches and pains wasn't explained.

The solution – according to American inventor Arthur Munchausen – was simple. Stop wearing enormous hats? No, that would be silly. Obviously, what was required was better air circulation.

So Arthur developed a network of metal rods, which was fixed to the wearer's shoulders. The hat could then be carefully positioned on top of the rods, so that it was just a little higher than usual, allowing the air to circulate freely between head and hat. Just in case people thought that a set of metal rods might look a bit unattractive, Arthur suggested they could be decorated with some nice ribbons. Sadly, no one liked his idea one little bit.

Meanwhile, what about the gentlemen? What if they got headaches from their hats, too? Well, they weren't forgotten. Another American inventor, Albert Eliel, came up with a head-mounted clockwork fan to suck cool air in under a hat brim. Brilliant. The weight, vibration, whirring noise, and frequent need to wind up the fan, not to mention the ever-present risk of a nasty tangle with one's hair, were no doubt all worth the lovely breeze.

ENCORE

In 1970 (and now, for that matter), opera-goers faced a number of problems – including where the best seats were, what to wear, and how to afford the tickets. It's probably safe to say, however, that an inability to clap loudly enough was not top of the list. Or, indeed, on the list. But, just in case it was, James Crawford had the answer: clapping gloves. There were several designs, and the gloves could be made of wood, metal or plastic, but they all worked in the same way – when clapped together, they made an extremely loud noise.

Inhuman inventions

Not all inventions are intended to make people's lives easier. Some have been dreamt up to bring a little something different into the lives of our pets.

Lots of animals – especially cats and dogs – enjoy a good back-scratching, but they often have owners who either don't know when that valuable service is required, or can't be bothered to provide it. But help is at hand from an inventor called David Haywood.

As soon as a cat or dog stands on a special platform, a robotic arm starts to move backwards and forwards. It has a specially designed 'hand' at the end, to deliver a really nice back-scratching. This would be ideal, if the cat or dog would stand in exactly the right place, and resist the urge to give the device a good scratch or bite.

After an experience like that, many dogs might want to leave the house – but how to let their owner know? Okay, there's whining, barking or whimpering, but they are all far too easy for humans to ignore. Doorbells, however, do usually get some attention, so Fred Amans came up with a special canine version. Since normal doorbells are rather a challenge for dogs, especially if their paws are a bit on the ginormous side, Fred came up with special scratching panels instead, one for each side of the door. All a bright dog needed to do was scratch and he'd be out – or in – in no time. Assuming, that is, he or she wasn't scratching just for scratching's sake. Which is not a very safe assumption.

There are also weird inventions for budgies and other caged birds, too. Life can be dull for them, with all that time spent sitting on a perch, tweeting. To change all that, William Dulle invented the rotating perch. Not at all dizzy-making or upsetting at all. Probably nice in the way that banging your head on a door is.

BAD TO WORSE

If you're sick or injured, the very last thing you'd want is to be put in an open box supported by four wobbly springs. About the only thing that could make the experience even more unpleasant is if the springs were attached to the saddle of a horse. Nevertheless, this was the fantastic idea of the even more fantastically named Hezekiah Thistle in 1837. He thought it would be a very handy way of getting people to hospital.

Fun on wheels

Wouldn't it be great to have a vehicle which needed no petrol, diesel, or electricity, and which was also very quiet? Isaac Smyth's gravity-car, invented in 1911, promised all of those things – with one small snag. To make it work, the driver had to spin a big wheel which – very slowly – lifted heavy weights into the air. When the weights were released, they descended, turning a system of gears attached to the wheels, so the car moved forward nicely. All was well until it needed 'refuelling' – by lifting the weights again. As this happened every few hundred metres or so, the novelty would probably have worn off quite rapidly.

Alternatively, motorists with dogs could take advantage of Mr May's 1870 invention: a carriage with a large drum at the front, which looked a little like a steamroller. The idea was that anyone who wanted to go for a spin would just pop their pooch into the drum and get him running, and away they'd go. It also worked with other pets. But not goldfish.

In the 19th century, giant swings were popular fairground rides. Several people would sit at either end, and pull ropes to make the gondola, as it was called, move from side to side. In 1895, a new version became available in Germany – one which could travel along roads. There was no steering wheel, but since the passengers at the front would be facing the wrong way, and would also block the view of those at the back, it wouldn't have been much use anyway.

EPILOGUE

Now that you know about some of the worst, weirdest, and wackiest inventions there are, you might want to try coming up with a brilliant invention of your own. Whether you actually build something, or simply design it, inventing things is great fun, and it might, just possibly, make you rich or famous, or both, one day. Have a go – all you need is an idea!

INVENTIONS IN QUESTION

Now that your mind is highly trained to appreciate the wonders and weirdness of inventions of all kinds, here's a little quiz. You'll find the answers on page 172.

1. What is a water closet?
A. a toilet.
B. a special fridge to keep chilled water.
C. a storage box for diving equipment.

2. A rockoon is:
A. an artificial moon, made of rock.
B. a robotic racoon.
C. a cross between a rocket and a balloon.

3. The first type of television to go on sale in the UK was called:
A. a televiewer.
B. a visilook.
C. a televisor.

4. The miner's friend was a 19th century:
A. magazine for miners to read.
B. steam-engine.
C. lamp for use underground.

5. An inventory is a:
A. list of things.
B. history of inventions.
C. workshop where things are invented.

6. What was voted the world's worst invention in 2007?
A. homework.
B. weapons.
C. sprouts.

7. What is a widget?
A. a mad-inventor cartoon character.
B. a thing that makes canned beer frothier.
C. a very small nut and bolt.

8. Mother's Day was invented sometime around 2,600 years ago. When was Father's day invented?
A. at about the same time.
B. in the 1800s.
C. in the 1900s.

9. Tim Berners-Lee invented the World Wide Web, one of the most successful inventions of the 20th century. Why didn't he patent it?
A. he wanted everyone to be able to use it.
B. patenting software isn't allowed.
C. he forgot.

10. The first ever story about a satellite was written in 1869. What was it made of?
A. bricks.
B. steel.
C. antigravity metal.

11. Thomas Edison was one of the greatest, if not THE greatest inventor ever. He said invention was 1% inspiration and 99%:
A. luck.
B. perspiration.
C. trial and error.

12. Why was the countdown for space launches invented?

A. so that the astronauts would know when lift-off would take place.

B. to make a film about space travel more exciting.

C. to make sure the rocket communication systems were working correctly.

13. Roughly how many patents are granted worldwide per year?

A. 8,000.

B. 80,000.

C. 800,000.

14. When was ice cream invented?

A. the 1710s.

B. the 1810s.

C. the 1910s.

ANSWERS:

1.A, 2.C, 3.C, 4.B, 5.A, 6.B, 7.B, 8.C, 9.A, 10.A, 11.B, 12.B, 13.C, 14.A.

172

LOOK out FOR